TRIUMPH
B O O K S

MARIÁN
HOSSA

MARIÁN HOSSA

My Journey from Trenčín
to the Hall of Fame

Marián Hossa
with Scott Powers

TRIUMPH
BOOKS

Library of Congress Cataloging-in-Publication Data for the hardcover edition is available upon request.

This book is available in quantity at special discounts for your group or organization. For further information, contact:

Triumph Books LLC
814 North Franklin Street
Chicago, Illinois 60610
(312) 337-0747
www.triumphbooks.com

Printed in U.S.A.
ISBN: 978-1-63727-454-5
Design by Patricia Frey

Photos courtesy of Marián Hossa unless otherwise indicated

Foreword

by Joel Quenneville

When I think of Marián Hossa, I think of the perfect hockey player—no maintenance, smart, comes to play every night, plays the right way, plays in all situations. We had some different kinds of players on our Blackhawks teams, but he was the one guy that would always be doing the right things in all areas. You were almost spoiled that you had him on your team knowing that. Sometimes you might have even overlooked him or just taken for granted that he was always getting the job done.

Before I coached him, I always thought he was a good player. I had coached against him when he was with Ottawa, Atlanta, and Detroit. You knew he did some things that not many guys can do when he put his stick down and protected the puck. You just couldn't touch it because he was so strong on his stick and the puck wasn't coming out of that area. I liked how he prepared and knowing that he got the job done. It was pretty amazing coming from Detroit and Pittsburgh and how many Cup finals he had been to in a row. After us, he was in five Cup finals in eight years, pretty amazing stuff. He was always a key factor. He was such an important guy on your team. You never had to worry about him not being ready to go, or that something's wrong with Hoss. He just did his job quietly and in the right way. I think he always was the most respected guy because he was such a nice, classy player, a classy guy. He wasn't one of the louder guys in the room, but he brought that professionalism that was important to our team.

I think back to when he got hit by Raffi Torres in that 2012 Phoenix series. That might have been the maddest I have been in a hockey game on the bench. Just knowing that when you lose him, your opportunity is going to be limited. It turned out it was. But it was good to see him come back after that.

In 2013, he missed Game 3 of the Stanley Cup Final against the Bruins with an injury. He came back in Game 4, and what a difference it was. We had some guys playing through different kinds of injuries. He was very upfront about it, and told me, "Hey, I'm limited. I can only do this." I trusted his input and decision-making in doing what was best for the team. He was limited, but he was still giving it everything. He still did everything right, and it was a big factor. In that series, I don't think people gave us a chance when we were down 2–1. He came back and we won three games in a row. I think his contribution meant a lot to the team. It wasn't just every shift on the ice that he played, but it was just his presence alone, and doing the right things. You know, Games 5 and 6 could have gone either way.

It was an easy decision for me to put together Hoss and Jonathan Toews on a line. You had Jonny who had the puck a lot. You had Hoss who had the puck a lot. You had the intensity, the consistency. The matchups, the importance of that line, winning the chance battles, outscoring the opposition, they were definitely influential in winning the game. I think certain individuals play the game to score points or get goals. Those two guys played to *win the game*, and I think as a coach you don't have a bigger appreciation for anything than that. I think that makes a big difference, having players that make the team the priority.

We obviously knew about his skin condition. We just basically left it to him if he wanted to practice. If you don't think it's a good idea, don't skate today. He basically had carte blanche. I think everyone respected him and understood he was doing what was best for the team and his health. Not too many players had that kind of pass with me.

When Hoss ultimately decided to retire, I thought we missed a lot of pace and continuity to our game. He was just so consistent. He was good shift after shift and always did the right thing. He was the captain in providing that type of assuredness. And then all of a sudden, it was sporadic. We still had great leaders and great guys around the team, but I thought he was always the most consistent in playing the right way.

I was honored and flattered that Hoss asked me to write this. I think it's a great, great honor. I've been fortunate to coach special players and some of the game's best, and he's a part of that. I wish him nothing but the best. He's a tremendous man, a tremendous family man, and the Slovakians got a special, special hockey player.

Introduction

Picture a young Marián Hossa coming home from a long day of school in Slovakia. Hockey, of course, was on my mind. We lived in very plain-looking, Communist-era apartment buildings in Trenčín, and outside was a playground where all the kids gathered to play hockey. My brother, Marcel, and I would be among the kids out there competing every day for our make-believe Stanley Cup. One day I would bring the real thing back to the same neighborhood. But I'm getting ahead of myself.

So, young Marián Hossa comes home from school—what do I do first? I don't actually remember this myself, but my mom, Mária, says my priority when I got home was always to fold my clothes nicely and put them on top of each other. If you knew me, which hopefully you will after reading this book, that wouldn't be surprising. I'm that way now as an adult and apparently was that same way as a kid.

I'm mostly a pretty easygoing person. You can ask all my former teammates and coaches. As Patrick Kane will tell you later, I'm someone you probably wouldn't mind sitting next to in the dressing room. I like to have fun, have a laugh, and just an overall good time. But when it comes to my business, which was previously playing hockey and is now actually real businesses, I liked to be more serious and definitely prepared. I've always believed you have a better chance of success if you're prepared, and that's how I always approach everything. Part of that is being organized.

So, yes, I like to have my clothes folded and in a certain place. I like to be organized. I want to know exactly what I'm getting into, whether it's purchasing a new household appliance or investing in a business. For example, my wife, Jana, recently wanted a new vacuum, a smaller one, for the kitchen, so she wouldn't have to pull out the larger one every time she needed it. I wanted to do some research before we bought one. There was one from a German company, Miele, I thought was the best from what I had read, but she liked another one. She's like, "Jesus Christ, I can't even buy the vacuum I like." I told her you can buy the one you like, for sure, but I was going to buy the Miele one as well, because I knew it was better. She responded, we don't need two vacuums in the kitchen. So, we bought the vacuum I liked, and it's great. When it comes to these types of gadgets, I know what I like. Don't get me wrong, when it comes to strollers or kids' stuff, she can pick anything and I won't interfere at all. It's her choice all the way.

As an NHL player, I prepared for big games in that same fashion. If we were playing against Scott Stevens and the New Jersey Devils, I read the scouting reports and looked for his weaknesses. What can I do against him? Maybe I can use my speed behind him? If I try to go at him direct, he's probably going to hit me so hard. Basically, I wanted to prepare the best I could to be successful on the ice. Even with something as simple as offseason workouts, I tried to stick to exactly what the plan was going into it. The attention to detail was crucial for me. If I didn't follow the details or skipped a workout, it would eat me up. I honestly wouldn't be able to sleep at night.

THROUGHOUT THIS BOOK, my co-author, Scott Powers, talked to various people I'm close to in my life, and you'll hear from them in different chapters. They'll help give you a better idea of who I was as a hockey player but also who I am as a son, brother, husband, father, friend, and teammate. For example, I asked Scott to talk to Peter Neveriš, who is one of my best friends and my agent in Slovakia.

"In this book, you'll probably find out how great Marián Hossa is," Peter said. "Surely, there will be words such as friendly, witty, precise, hardworking, purposeful, empathetic, polite, humane, faithful, conscious, appreciative, but at the same time experienced and certainly much more. As a person who has known Marián since the age of six and still has a strong friendship with him, I can tell you with all seriousness that these are all true words. And it's not just because the book is supposed to tell you mostly nice things, but mainly because he really is like that.

"If you asked Marián who his best friend was, I guess he would hardly say only one name. And if you asked me one word that characterizes Marián, then there would have to be two: humility and character. Marián is a person whose fame, success, and money have absolutely not changed him. He is still the same great person who, when he meets you on the street, is the first to greet you. He has a moral code that includes treating other people with respect.

"Nowadays, it is very rare for someone to say something and actually mean it. Marián doesn't say empty words and always keeps his promises. He's a man of his word. His charisma and character make him a personality who we know and admire."

No one knows me, or what I'm like to live with, better than my wife. To get a better idea of my organizational tactics, here's what Jana said about me: "He always followed his schedule with his habits and exercise and everything. He was never like, OK, I'm tired, so I won't go to practice, or, I'll cut it by an hour. Even in the summer, I sometimes asked him to just skip one. He was always like, no. He had to keep his schedule organized. That's the way he's always been."

I don't know where it comes from, maybe my parents. My little brother was different. We shared a bedroom, and one half of the closet would be really organized, and his would be a little messy. (He has gotten neater with age.) It's tough to say why I was that way, but it has carried over throughout the rest of my life. I know if I stick to the plan and stay organized that I'll likely be successful. There have been times where I haven't been as prepared, and I could feel something was wrong. I wouldn't be as confident and comfortable. I felt like I shorted myself. That's why I've always tried to not feel that way.

Preparation was essential as I was planning my career and trying to win the real Stanley Cup. When I was set to become a free agent after the 2007–08 season, my agent, Ritch Winter, and I created a plan for me, so I could be successful throughout the rest of my career. I took charge of my own path. Ritch put together a book of possible teams I could sign with and laid out salary caps, projected lineups, and where I could fit in. The book let me envision my options in the short and long term. That was what I needed as guidance to help me make my decision.

First, I surprised most people and signed with the Detroit Red Wings on a one-year deal. Everyone assumes I did that in an attempt to win the Stanley Cup, especially after losing the season before with the Pittsburgh Penguins. Yes, of course, I wanted to win. Who wouldn't want to win? But that wasn't the whole story. You'll have to keep reading to find out why I went to Detroit and played with all those future Hall of Famers. After Detroit, I signed a 12-year contract with the Chicago Blackhawks. Again, I took a lot of time to research where I best fit, who had up-and-coming stars, and which team might allow me to finally lift that Stanley Cup.

Unfortunately, I wasn't able to play out my contract with the Blackhawks because of my skin condition. It's one of the many subjects we'll dive deeper into throughout this book. It was tough because I walked away from the game when I felt like I could still play at a high level. Transitioning to a non-hockey life was easier than I expected. I finally didn't have somewhere I needed to be at an exact time. I was able to finally enjoy having some flexibility in my life, and being able to spend more time with Jana and our two daughters, Mia and Zoja.

We returned to Slovakia from Chicago and began a new chapter in our life. I have rediscovered that structure through a few different businesses I own here. It's a nice mixture of enjoying life, traveling with my family, hanging out with

Marcel and my friends, but also getting down to business when needed. Just like I did as that young kid coming home from school or as an NHL player playing in the Stanley Cup Final, I still try to be as prepared and organized as I can. For me, it's just one of those necessary ingredients to a successful life.

One

Before my NHL career ever began, I was worried it was over.

I was pretty fortunate not to suffer too many injuries in my career. There was my skin condition that forced me into retirement, and I'll expand on that later, but I never really thought of that as an injury. If we're talking about real injuries, the worst one I had occurred before I became an everyday NHL player.

I was drafted by the Ottawa Senators as the 12th overall pick in 1997 and joined them for their training camp in the fall. I played really well at camp and was scoring goals. I think I impressed them as an 18-year-old. With my play and Daniel Alfredsson holding out for a new contract at that time, they decided to keep me on their NHL roster to start the season. But then I wasn't as productive when the season began, and especially when Alfredsson finally signed, the Senators decided they were going to re-assign me. The Portland Winterhawks had selected me in the CHL import draft and held my rights there. They had actually traded up to draft me. I'm not exactly sure why, but it worked out.

I was disappointed to be leaving Ottawa. I remember the media asked me how I felt, and I said, in my broken English, "I'll be back." One newspaper used that quote the next day as if I was Arnold Schwarzenegger saying, "I'LL BE BACK" in *The Terminator*. What I meant was, I'd play in the WHL but count on me returning to the NHL. Going to Portland was difficult to swallow at the time, but it ended up being the right decision. I can't argue with it now. I learned a lot on and off the ice playing in Portland. I scored 58 goals and produced 104 points in 69 games between the regular season and play-offs and was voted the league's rookie of the year. We went on a playoff run, won the WHL championship, and reached the Memorial Cup Final in Spokane, Washington.

My injury happened in the final game of the Memorial Cup. We were playing the Guelph Storm. They had Manny Malhotra. It was a pretty even game. We were tied 3–3 with about five minutes left in the third period. I had the puck and was entering the blue line near the left boards. I was cutting in after crossing the blue line. There were two defensemen waiting for me. One of them started charging me and I made a move on him. I got past him, but he stuck out his knee and caught my left knee. I went flying in the air like a helicopter. When I landed, I knew right away something was wrong. I had never been hurt like that before. I remember yelling as I was lying on the ice. I was holding my knee and felt this terrible pain. I knew my knee was done. The Storm player was called for a game misconduct penalty. The trainer came onto the ice and I was helped off.

I sat in the dressing room and watched the rest of the game. I was sitting there and took a look at my knee. The first thing I thought was, well, I hope we win this game. Second, I started thinking about my career. I was drafted early by the Senators. I had already played some NHL games. I was playing in the Memorial Cup and had played well that season. I had also won the championship with Dukla back home the season before. So everything was going really well for me up to that point. And then all of a sudden, I suffered this injury. I had never experienced anything like that. I was painting the worst pictures in my head. "This could happen or that could happen." There were so many questions going through my head.

We did end up winning the game. Bobby Russell scored on a rebound in overtime. Sitting in the dressing room alone, watching the overtime in pain, for a split second, I started yelling, "Goaaaallll! We won!" Our trainer Innes Mackey ran in to celebrate with me and helped me join my teammates on the ice. I was wearing my jersey and only had on flipflops. They put me in a chair and the guys pushed me around the ice as I carried the Cup. Later in the hotel, they put my chair on the luggage cart and pushed me around on that.

The injury tested me in a way that I hadn't been tested before, but that also turned out to be a positive. More on that soon. But being in Portland and playing for the Winterhawks were experiences that I'll forever cherish. When I arrived in Portland, it helped that I already knew a few people. One of Portland's assistants was Július Šupler, who I had known since I was a kid in Slovakia. He coached with my dad on Dukla Trenčín and the national team. Julo was a big shot in Slovakia and a well-respected coach for taking Slovak hockey from C category to A category in two years. He had decided to go to North America to be an assistant and try to learn some new things. There was also a Slovakian player, Andrej Podkonický, who was on the team. He was an assistant coach on the Slovakia national team that won a bronze medal at the 2022 Olympics. They both helped my transition to a new team.

I had been given a billet family to stay with, Linda and Rich Donaldson, in Portland. They were an older couple, really nice. Their kids were grown up and out of the house. They owned an older home in a quiet neighborhood. I came to Portland a little bit after the start of the season, so they already had a player living with them. That ended up being Brenden Morrow. We had rooms next each other in their big basement, which had a walk-out patio. We basically had our

Celebrating winning the Memorial Cup with my Portland teammates

living room downstairs and would play video games there. It was a nice setup. Brenden helped me a lot in the beginning. My English wasn't great, and he'd spend time talking with me. Looking back, it probably wasn't easy for him to have me as a roommate. It was probably a little challenging at times. But he was great to me. We still keep in touch to this day. We obviously saw a lot of each other in the NHL, especially when he was the captain of the Dallas Stars. In his final season with the Tampa Bay Lightning, I played him in the Stanley Cup Final. Andrew Ference was one of our defensemen on that Portland team, and I'd later play him in the Stanley Cup Final when he was with the Boston Bruins.

Brent Peterson was the coach of the Winterhawks. He later became an assistant for the Nashville Predators. We had a great relationship, too, and talked whenever we saw each other throughout our careers. I thought he was a really good coach and understood hockey really well. The Winterhawks had great coaching and a talented team. They were winning before I got there. I joined them and we didn't lose many games. I had a lot of fun that season. As I said, I didn't want to go to Portland at first, but it was good for me. I scored a lot of goals and gained confidence. We won the Memorial Cup. I also enjoyed myself off the ice, with the long trips and being around the guys.

It was while I was in Portland that my first NHL check arrived. It was my signing bonus, and the check got mailed to the Donaldsons' address. They opened the mail and showed it to me. They're like, "Marián, you got a check for something like $200,000." They started panicking and now I understand why, but back then, I was like, "Hmmmm, can I just finish my video game, please?" They didn't know what to do with it and were scared to lose it. I told them in my broken English that I didn't know what to do with it either. I was 18 years old and just had this money on paper. They recommended opening a checking account. I called my agent and asked for his advice. We eventually got me an account.

My agent had asked before if there was anything I'd like to buy when I signed my first contract. My dream car was always a 911 Turbo Porsche. He was like, that's a great dream, but it might not look good if you're on this junior team driving around in a Porsche. He said I should wait until I got to the NHL, but I didn't buy it then either. I thought, maybe when I score 500 goals or reach 1,000 games, but to this day, I still haven't bought it. But now that I have officially retired from the NHL as a Blackhawk, I believe it is the right time to get my dream car.

What I drove in Portland was a Ford Expedition. All my junior teammates had like these small cars, and I showed up with this huge truck, fully loaded. I'd be driving all the guys around in this big truck. I have a lot of great memories from that time.

Marshall Johnston

It goes back, goes back a long way. I was over in what was at that time Czechoslovakia, and now, of course, it's just Slovakia. Anyway, I'm guessing he was about maybe 14 years old or so. I was over there looking at the senior team and his dad was the assistant coach of that team. I was looking at older players, but I didn't have much to do before the senior team games. I used to go there and these little kids, probably 14 or so, they come across the road from this school which was only about a block and a half away. They'd be coming across from school around 2:30 or so and practice, and then after they were done, the senior team would practice. So I got to know his dad and met Marián. And then, of course, as Marián got older, I used to see him in tournaments, like the junior tournaments, and he was going to make the World juniors team for his country.

His skills were all good, but he played a two-way game. He wasn't all fancy. He was a backchecker. He was just a complete, complete player. And I'm not sure what it was, I mean, truthfully, I had no idea when we drafted him that he was going to be as good as he was. I had no idea. I'd be lying if I said, oh, yeah, I could see him 20 years from now in the Hockey Hall of Fame. I can't tell you that. I'm not that smart. But when you hook onto somebody and then when I saw him around Ottawa and the respect he had from his teammates and everything, he just stood out.

One

It was the 1997 draft in Pittsburgh, if I'm not mistaken. I wasn't the manager of the team. I was director of player personnel. He was the guy that we wanted, for sure. So the manager asked, well, who do we like, this and that, and the manager told me, I think we got a chance to get him. We were picking at No. 12. I was sweating bullets, because like I said, we really liked him. I quite honestly was on pins and needles during the first round. We wanted him that bad, but I wasn't sure if he'd get to No. 12. I thought he might be gone. So when he was there, there was no deliberating. He was the one.

The next year, the coach of Slovakia's national senior team, Július Šupler, went over to America to coach the junior team in Portland. So we thought it would be advantageous if Marián came over there and got used to playing in North American rinks and so on, and so he did. It helped him because he could only speak some English back then. The team did very well. They were in the Memorial Cup finals, and Marián tore up his knee and had to be operated on. I remember flying out there to see him and we arranged for the operation with Ottawa. The next year after he got healed up, he started playing with the Senators. We had some good drafts during those years and some trades and so on, and the team was doing very well, but I left; I had a disagreement with the president of the team and the owner.

I always kept in touch with Marián. Usually at Christmastime before he got married, I'd send him a Christmas card and he'd always reply back to me. And, of course, he got married and got those two pretty little girls and wife. We happened to go to Slovakia and

11

Trenčín, me and my wife, and we looked him up and he invited us over for dinner with his family. And then I was really blessed when he invited us to come to his Hockey Hall of Fame induction. We felt very privileged. He wanted to pay for the hotel and he wanted to pay for the airfare. But fortunately, we were in a position I just got to be there. I wasn't concerned about the expenses, and he ended up having us to his dinner with his agent, Dominik Hašek, Nick Lidström, and all his friends and family who had come over from Slovakia. It was terrific.

Two

Starting my NHL career in Ottawa was perfect for me in a lot of ways. I have a lot of great memories playing in that city. It never felt too big or overwhelming. It had a European feel, similar to cities I was familiar with back home. On and off the ice, I enjoyed playing in Ottawa and for the Senators. I wish things hadn't ended how they did. The end of my time there left a bad taste in my mouth.

Before we get to the end, let's talk about my beginning in Ottawa. After being injured in the Memorial Cup, I had surgery to repair my ACL, which I still have a scar from. The doctor did an excellent job and promised it would be strong again. We came up with a plan for rehab and decided I would stay in Ottawa for the offseason. I actually don't know if they gave me an option to rehab in Slovakia. My English wasn't that great then, so I said yes to everything. I did go home for a week and packed my bags. My mom returned with me to Ottawa and helped me for a few months. She drove me around and everything. I was still just 18. It took me some time to make friends and eventually get to know some people in the hockey circle. There were also some other players staying for the summer. I was on crutches and they'd invite me out to eat. It was a fun time becoming an NHL player and living in a Canadian city.

The rehab process was different than anything I was used to coming from Europe. We didn't put ice on our body in Europe like they did in North America. I had to learn to accept having ice on my knee. The first time, they put a bag of ice on the front of my knee and another on the back of it and told me to keep them there for 20 minutes. After two minutes, I nearly fainted and started taking them off. They asked me what I was doing and I told them I was going to die. It was too cold. It took me a week or so to get used to it; my skin would turn red because it was so cold. Nowadays, they do the same in Europe, but not back then. We might have had a cold spray, but nothing like those ice bags or cold tubs. But I listened to them and believed they knew what they were doing. They said it would help me heal quicker, so that's what I did. But that cold sensation definitely took me some time to get used to. Later in my career, I remember Blackhawks teammate Brent Sopel would have ice bags just on one side of his body because he'd always block shots on that side. He'd be walking naked through the room and one side of his body looked normal and the other was all blue. He was the one who wore the most ice bags in 2010. In 2013, it was Michal Handzuš, who seemed like he was sleeping in the cold tub.

Looking back at what happened, there was something good that came out of the whole ACL injury. I was a skinny kid back then. I was talented, but I was really skinny. At that time in the National Hockey League, you had to be physically ready to play at that level. It's not like now where you have skinny guys skating, turning and everything. You had to be strong in front of the net. There were people hacking and whacking at you. I was skilled and offensive-minded, but it would have been tough to play 82 games. I wouldn't have gotten strong enough to handle that if I hadn't suffered that injury. I also wouldn't have stayed in Ottawa that off-season and would have returned to Slovakia. I would have trained back home, but it wouldn't have been the same and I would still have been that skinny kid. I also trusted the people who were taking care of me, so I stopped worrying about my future. I was able to erase all those questions I had back at the Memorial Cup about my career. I knew I was in good hands. I also started to see progress. I could feel myself getting more muscular. I knew I was headed in a good direction.

I really worked hard with our conditioning coach, Randy Lee, to become bigger and stronger. I spent most of the days in the gym working on my core and upper body with Randy. I'd have my mom drop me off and pick me up in three or four hours. I didn't have much else to do. I gained a lot of weight and got a lot stronger. Once I started playing again, I didn't feel like anyone could put me down. I felt like I was so much more prepared mentally and physically to play in the NHL. I remember playing Mats Sundin and the Maple Leafs, and I had hit somebody, and Sundin came up to me and said, "Hoss, get off the juice." He couldn't believe how much stronger I had gotten. I'm like, "Yeah, Mats, whatever." I was just a kid still. I had lot of respect for Mats, he was superstar, but I didn't care what he was thinking. It was just hard work and a lot of hours in the gym.

Most of my experiences with the Senators were great. I played for them for six seasons, seven if you count my seven games in the 1997–98 season. I have so many memories from that time. I'll never forget going to Florida for the first time and scoring my first NHL goal in the third period against the Panthers. Alexei Yashin set me up perfectly at the net. That puck is on my wall at home right next to my 500th career goal.

I was young in Ottawa and we were a young team overall. I was living a dream. I was playing in the NHL and having a blast. I started hanging out with Marty Havlát and Radek Bonk.

Marty was especially young, and we did a lot together because we were both single. After games, we'd go out for dinner or we'd head to the club to have some fun if it was the right time. I remember our coach, Jacques Martin, put the three of us on a power play and we had so much fun. We scored a lot of goals together. Our captain, Daniel Alfredsson, was on the blue line.

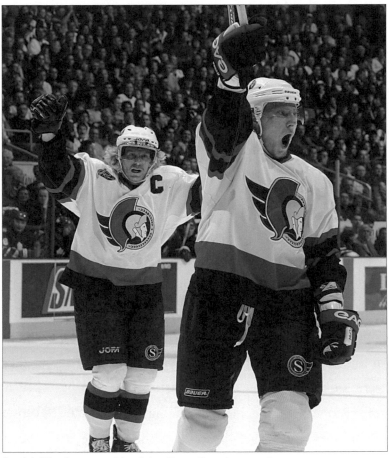

Daniel Alfredsson and I celebrating a Senators goal *(Getty Images)*

He was a great player and a fantastic person. We were winning a lot, plus we did enjoy being together. What else could you wish for when you're in your 20s and playing in the best league in the world?

Jacques Martin was good for me as my first NHL coach. He was all about the details, and I didn't have a problem with that at all. That fit how I like to do things, that organizational part of my mind, as I explained earlier. I think he trusted me from the beginning, too, and that's why he was willing to play me at such a young age. I came into the league as more of an offensive player, but I started learning more about defensive play under Jacques. It would be later in my career that I'd become a true two-way forward, but some of those lessons began in Ottawa.

I played with Radek Bonk for a long time with the Senators. It was Bonk, Magnus Arvedson, and me on a line. We started as the third line, but we produced a lot. Bonk was a left-handed center, and that began a long run of lefty centers for me in the NHL. I always liked to play with a left-handed center as a right winger because they'd get the puck in the middle and I'd be the first person they'd see as they were looking to their right. Decisions need to be made in split seconds in this game, and having that left-handed center could allow me to get the puck while skating with speed. Bonk was a bigger guy, so he wasn't the fastest, but he saw the ice really well and made smart plays. He could score too. Before he was drafted to the NHL, he was playing in Vegas in the IHL and scored a lot of goals there. When I joined the Senators, they put us on a line and we worked well together.

One of my favorite road trip stories came while in Ottawa. We were in California, and I must have been 22, 23 years old. After an afternoon game, we had the next day off, and some of the guys went out for dinner. We then decided to go to a club, and outside was a long, white Mercedes S-Class with flames painted around the whole car. It was really unique. We asked the bouncer whose car it was, and the bouncer said it was Dennis Rodman's. He owned the club.

There were probably seven or eight of us players. We got a table and some beers. There was a band playing on the club's stage. I then saw Rodman by the bar, and I'm like, wow, that's pretty cool. THE Dennis Rodman that I was watching in the NBA was now in the same club as me. So cool. I watched him as he walked over to the band, grabbed the microphone from the singer in the middle of their song, and said, "You guys are done." The music stopped and no one knew what was going on. He's like, "I told you guys, get out. I'll still pay you anyway, motherfuckers." Those were his words. I still remember that to this day. They were all surprised. He just kicked them out and told the DJ to start playing music.

He later walked over to us and asked us where we were from. We told him we were players from the National Hockey League. He's like, "Welcome. You guys want to do something?" One of our tough guys, André Roy, was there. He was a big guy who could fight when necessary, but he was a really funny guy too. He put some salt on the table and started pretending to do a line. Dennis was like, "You want some? I got some." Andre's like, no, I was just kidding. I'm like, holy shit.

We finished the last beers in our bucket, and Shawn McEachern pretended like he was going to put the bucket over his head. Dennis came over there and was like, "Do it. Fucking do it." Shawn's looking at him just amazed. He's like, no, I was just joking. So Dennis grabbed the bucket full of ice and water and flipped it over his own head. He's like, "Yeah, that's how we do it, motherfucker." I couldn't believe it. He then got free drinks with us. You always heard how hard he partied, but I learned that was basically true. He was unreal.

As a team, we had some success in Ottawa. Our problem was we just couldn't get past Toronto most seasons. We could beat the Maple Leafs in the regular season anytime. But in the playoffs, they had our number. I lost to the Leafs four times in the playoffs while with Ottawa. They had a tough team with Domi, Corson, Tucker, Belak, McCabe, Roberts. They had a big team, were fast and skilled. With the old rules of clutching and grabbing, it was difficult to beat them because of the size and toughness they had. We did nearly go to the Stanley Cup Final one season. We reached the Eastern Conference Final in 2003 and lost to the New Jersey Devils in seven games.

I was planning to remain in Ottawa for longer than I did. I was hoping to sign an extension when I became a restricted free agent after the 2003–04 season. I was coming off a season where I scored 36 goals and produced a point per game. I had 45 goals the season before. John Muckler was the GM of the Senators at the time and he knew I wanted to re-sign. But he wasn't willing to pay me the salary a player at my level warranted, even though I was producing a lot. My agent then, Jiří Crha, said we could choose to go to arbitration. I was like, "Yes, for sure."

I thought they loved me in Ottawa. I really liked it there, too, and wanted to stay. But the Senators had different plans. I just didn't know about them yet.

While I was thinking about re-signing, they had already been talking to the Atlanta Thrashers. Muckler really like Dany Heatley, who played for Atlanta. So Muckler already had this deal in his back pocket. My agent and I flew to Toronto to meet with him and Peter Chiarelli for the arbitration hearing. My goal was to get $6 million a year. I didn't know it then either, but Atlanta apparently told Ottawa that $6 million was also the maximum they'd be willing to pay me.

That morning, right before we went to court, Muckler sent my agent a text saying that he and Chiarelli wanted to meet with us. We agreed and met in a really small room. They said they'd give me $6 million. I didn't understand it. I had flown all the way from Slovakia to Toronto, and now they were going to give me this deal? Why not tell me when I was back home? I started getting the sense that something wasn't right. My agent told them to put a no-trade clause in the contract, and Muckler said he never did that. That told me something right there. I told my agent, if somebody doesn't want me, I don't want to be there. But I did agree to the deal.

Chiarelli opened up a bag and he had like a big fax machine in it. I'm like, "Wow, that's a jumbo fax machine. Is this normal?" So, I signed the deal in this small room right before my arbitration hearing and we shook hands. They then said they had to do something there and we could go. They thanked us and said they'd see me at camp. I told my agent that all of it felt weird. He agreed, but he said we got the deal we wanted and that's great.

I went to the airport to fly back to Slovakia, and I got a call from my teammate Marty Havlát. He told me he was hearing rumors on the radio that Ottawa was going to trade me. I'm like, "Oh, here we go." I told him how the meeting went and that I wouldn't be surprised if that happened. And it did. I was sitting on the plane and Muckler's name showed up on my phone. He's like, "Marián, just wanted to tell you that we've traded you to the Atlanta Thrashers." I'm like, "Wow, just like that? Well, OK, bye." I didn't tell him anything else. It bothered me that my agent didn't know about it at all. I felt like he could have done something more.

That was the first time I tasted that side of the NHL business. I had been in Ottawa for seven seasons and I was like a piece of cheese to them. I had scored 40-plus goals and had all these points, and they traded me just like that. I had nine hours of flight time ahead of me, so I had plenty of time to think about everything that had happened. I came to realize the National Hockey League is a big business, and there are some people who just don't care how you feel. It made me stronger. I just had to take it.

Flash forward to my first game back in Ottawa after being traded to Atlanta. After the game, I was standing in the hallway chatting with some Senators players. There were maybe five or seven of us in a circle. I then saw Muckler walking through the hallway. He stopped and tapped me on the shoulder. I looked over and he had his hand out for me to shake it. I just let him hold it there. I turned back around to the guys and kept talking. He stood there for a few moments with his hand in the air. He finally got the message and walked away. I wanted to get across, hey, buddy, you didn't handle things the right way, and also like, fuck off. It bothered me for some time. Eventually, I did get over it.

GOING FROM OTTAWA, a Canadian hockey city, an "A" market, to Atlanta, a team in the South of the U.S., a "C" market team, was somewhat of a culture shock. I remember getting to Atlanta and there wasn't any water or Gatorade in the refrigerator. I was also told I should only use my new hockey sticks for the games, not for the practices. These were things I had never heard before. I was like, "Geez, this is the National Hockey League?" From the first moment, it was different for me. But I got to know the trainers and I liked them. I then started scoring goals and they decided, "Hoss, you can have a stick when you need a stick." But there was still no water in the fridge. When I asked why, they told me it was because guys were taking them home and the budget was too small for that. I didn't realize hockey markets could be so totally different.

I remember trying to order cable while in Atlanta. I called and a lady picked up the phone and I couldn't understand her deep Southern accent. She was nice, but I couldn't understand her. She probably thought I was stupid because I kept asking her to repeat herself. I felt bad. After like 10 tries, I hung up. I redialed and just prayed I'd get someone else.

It was really difficult in the beginning in Atlanta. But I got to like the city. There were some different opportunities in the

24

city to attend basketball and football games. As for hockey, I decided to go with the flow and focus on my game and not worry about how everything else was different.

Bob Hartley was the coach in Atlanta. He had a similar personality to Mike Babcock, who I would play for later in my career with Detroit. Bob was really tough on the young players and he knew how to really squeeze everything out of you. But if you played the right way, he liked you. He and Ilya Kovalchuk had some exchanges on the bench. Kovy would do what he wanted to do. He was also one of the most talented players I ever played with. He could skate forever and dance with the puck like no one else. He had a laser for a shot too. He was fun to watch. There were times when he'd had enough of Bob and kept scoring goals anyway. But Bob wasn't afraid to show Kovy who the boss was either.

Bob could also be a little sarcastic in certain ways. He always had tough camps and practices. I remember my buddy Milan Bartovič, who was a very fast skater, was invited to one camp. Bob came up to me and asked who would win in a race, Milan or Jimmy Slater, another very fast player. I told him it would be very close. Bob had this super tough drill that was called "mountain." You'd go from the goal line to the blue line and then back to the goal line, until you went from goal line to goal line. Bob was strict about the drill. You couldn't turn when skating. You had to stop. He would have trainers on the ice to patrol the lines to keep an eye on whether guys were stopping. So, he put Barts and Slates beside each other. Bob skated to one of the lines to make sure they didn't cheat, but he then skated to me and said, "Hoss, tell your boy he can cheat on his wife, but not me." I started laughing so hard.

Bob had some great jokes, but he was tough. Sometimes we'd be watching tape, and he'd have the remote in his hand and stop the tape. He'd turn to a young player and ask, "Is this your best effort?" The young guys wouldn't know what to say. If they said yes, Bob would say, "Really? *This* is your best effort?" If they said no, Bob would say, "Why aren't you giving your best effort?" There was no right answer. He knew that too.

There was this one time where we had a poor string of games. We were coming home to Atlanta late after one of these bad games. Usually after a road trip we would go back to our beds, get some sleep, then practice later the next day. This time Bob decided he wanted us to be at the rink at 7 a.m. He said he wanted us to experience what it was like to be regular people having to get up early and go to work. So we got home at 2 a.m. and would have to get up just a few hours later to get back to the rink. I remember it was one of the hardest practices we ever had. He made his point that this was how most people worked and we had these luxury lifestyles. That was Bob. He didn't bullshit anybody and he didn't give a shit. Everyone was tired because we obviously didn't get enough sleep, but he didn't care. He wanted to punish us. I thought Bob was a madman. I knew Bob was crazy, but this was nothing like I had ever experienced before. Afterward, we went out to breakfast and then everybody went back to bed.

I can't complain that much about Bob, though. He gave me plenty of opportunities. He knew he could trust me. I started really establishing myself as a goal scorer because I was getting that ice time. I could skate and then showed I could make moves on defensemen and goalies, and all of a sudden the goals were coming.

Don Waddell was the general manager in Atlanta at the time. He was a really nice guy and I had a great relationship with him. Even later when he had no option but to trade me to Pittsburgh, he was always great to me. Brad McCrimmon was an assistant coach for the Thrashers and one of my favorites of my career. I had him as an assistant in Detroit later too. I could talk with him for hours about hockey or life. We often had some good laughs. He was also there for me when the times weren't so easy.

I never scored 50 goals in my career. I had 45 one year in Ottawa and 43 another year in Atlanta. I did reach 100 points in my second season with the Thrashers. It's something not many players reach, so I was proud of that. I'm glad I got there once in my career. I also had a season in Atlanta where

I scored seven shorthanded goals. I had gotten pretty good at reading the game. Plus, I was in great shape. I'd make a read and outskate the opponents with my speed. I really started to enjoy playing the penalty kill. I found myself getting better chances to score on the PK than I did 5-on-5.

Bob liked to change the lines quite a bit, so I played with a lot of different players in Atlanta. We had a really strong power play. We had Slava Kozlov, Kovalchuk, Marc Savard, and there was a Swedish kid, Toby Enström. Kovy could score from anywhere. Koz and Marc Savard could pass the puck really well. Enström could see the ice really well. I was just around the post at the net. We were pretty successful on the power play.

Atlanta was also great for having a few of my countrymen on the team, like Bobby Holík. He was a beauty. He always wanted to drive and we lived in the same apartment complex. He'd drive me to games or the airport. He had this pickup truck. He was making millions of dollars and he had this pickup truck. I'd always give him shit: "You're making all this money. Why don't you have a Mercedes?" He was like, "Fuck that. I had a Mercedes and it was bad for my hips because it was too low. I like these big trucks." He didn't spend a lot of money on cars or clothes, but he would pay anything for food. He loved sushi. There were a lot of great restaurants in Atlanta. He could eat forever. We called him Big Diesel.

When the food was good, he tipped generously too. But when it came to clothes, I don't think he owned a pair of jeans. He was like a farmer and just a down-to-earth guy, quality guy. I loved him, and the way he talked was different than the other guys. He had won two Stanley Cups in New Jersey, so I'd ask him questions about those teams, coaches, and what it was like. He'd compared it to Atlanta where he was involved with some bad teams and felt like the coaches weren't making the right decisions. The way he said it in Czech was hilarious. We had a lot of good laughs. We also had a young Patrik Štefan, a former No. 1 pick; Ronald Petrovický, a Slovak; the great Peter Bondra; and Czech defenseman Jaroslav Modrý.

Back then, I was real particular about my stick and how I worked on it. I remember when it wasn't feeling right, I'd be taping the knob on the bench all the time. Bob Hartley would see that and yell, "Still playing with your fuckin' stick." I'd respond, "Don't worry about my stick, Bob, just put me out there."

It was in Atlanta where I went to buy my first iPhone. I've had many iPhones since, but none as memorable as the first. I was standing in line for the phone behind two young, skinny guys. They were looking at the phones on display. They then looked at each other and at the same time attempted to pull the phones off the display. One was able to, but the other couldn't get it. They both ran and one phone was left dangling from the cord. They were gone, so it was just me there standing with this phone swaying. The cops came and everything was explained. I eventually did get my iPhone.

Atlanta was also where I started my charity, HOSS Heroes. Other people mostly ran the charity at first and I would show up to events. I'd play street hockey with some kids. I remember taking a bunch of kids to the aquarium. It was a way for me to help underprivileged children. I could help put a smile on their faces. It felt good. We've continued to do the charity in Slovakia and I try to help out in the community as well.

I decided to change agents when I went to Atlanta for a number of reasons, not just because of how things ended in Ottawa. Jiří Crha, my former agent, used to be a goalie for the Toronto Maple Leafs. He's a Czech guy and I had known him since I was a kid. He was great. He's a nice guy and I had a good relationship with him and his wife, Marcela. I still keep in touch with him. But I knew sometimes you have to make difficult decisions in this business. My parents weren't happy when I left him because they liked him and knew him from the communist days. My parents are very old school like that. He had done a great job, but I felt I had elevated my game and I needed something different. I needed someone who could better negotiate what I needed. I was devasted going from a hockey market to a non-hockey market. I didn't want to leave Ottawa then. I had a lot of great friends and teammates there.

Two

I thought maybe an agent based in North America might be better too.

I had heard about Ritch Winter through someone. Ritch and I spoke on the phone a few times and he flew to Atlanta to meet me at a hotel. He had a lot of ideas and suggestions for me and my future. I liked him. He brought me a book that outlined players in different categories and what contracts could look like for me going forward. I explained to him my goals and how I eventually wanted to win a Stanley Cup. We talked a lot and created a bunch of ideas for my future. He did a lot of homework, and I had a clear picture of what was ahead. He wasn't just feeding me what I wanted to hear. He delivered what was real and possible for me. It was really detailed, and I really like people who are organized. It hit me that this guy was professional, organized, and a great communicator. I really liked him. When my contract in Atlanta expired, he became my agent, and he still is today. That was one of the best moves I made. I felt better positioned for my future and long-term success.

Three

The night before the 2008 Stanley Cup Playoffs began, I was in my Pittsburgh hotel room doing 500 squats. It had become my routine late that season. The night before a game, I'd knock them all out right before I went to sleep. Five-hundred squats goes by a lot faster than you'd think. I started doing them because I'd gotten hurt after being acquired by the Pittsburgh Penguins at the trade deadline from Atlanta, and figured there'd be some pressure on me when I got back into the lineup. They were expecting me to be a difference-maker and I wanted to come through. That night as I did my squats, I was hopeful for the playoffs. Sidney Crosby and I seemed to be creating some chemistry. The team was looking good. But I had no idea what was in store for all of us the next few months.

The idea for the squats came from Jaromír Jágr. I'll write even more about this later, but Marcel and I used to do Jágr's workout routine as kids. I figured the squats did Jags well during his days with the Penguins. To this day, I don't think Jags was telling the truth in his book. I actually believe he did 1,000 squats rather than the 500 he wrote about, because he was so much better and stronger than everyone else. The squats did make me feel pretty good late into that season. I felt stronger on the ice during that stretch, so I kept on doing them throughout the playoffs.

Being traded to the Penguins was exactly what I needed. I went from the Thrashers, a team that wasn't going to make the playoffs, to the Penguins, a really good team with a lot of potential. I always wanted to win throughout my NHL career, but it really became a priority during my time with Atlanta. I was in my ninth NHL season and had turned 29 during the 2007–08 season. Up to then, I had only gotten past the first round of the Stanley Cup Playoffs twice. I reached the second round in 2002 and the Eastern Conference Final in 2003. If I had gone to the Stanley Cup Final with Ottawa, or we had won it, maybe my career is different and I make different decisions later on. But in Atlanta, I started to focus more on winning. I had a 100-point season with the Thrashers, which was great, and I was playing a lot of minutes and felt like I was really important, but we simply weren't winning. As cool as it is to score 40-something goals and have 100 points, I wanted to win. The Stanley Cup was what became my driving force.

It's what I sought to accomplish more than anything in my career.

With my contract expiring after the 2007–08 season and the Thrashers getting swept in the first round the year before, I told their owners I would only consider re-signing if they brought in some more quality players to give us a chance to go further in the playoffs. The Thrashers weren't going to bring anyone in. I knew that. They knew that. So, they traded me. The trade came on February 26, 2008, the day of the deadline. We were in Montreal about to play the Canadiens. I went to breakfast in the morning at the team hotel, but I was then told not to leave for the morning skate. I knew the trade was coming. I was sitting in my room and then all of a sudden Don Waddell called me. He's like, "Marián, we got you a new team, it's the Pittsburgh Penguins." In my mind, I went, yes, wow. I knew they were a great team. Mario Lemieux, one of my childhood idols, was one of their owners. They had Sidney Crosby, Evgeni Malkin, and a talented group around them. I was excited. I'm not going to lie, as I was sitting in my hotel room, my heart started racing. I didn't know many people in Pittsburgh, maybe a few of the older players from the Czech Republic, but I was really excited and looking forward to getting there.

I could quickly tell the Penguins organization was at a different level. Mario sent a private jet for us. I was traded with

Pascal Dupuis. He joked, "I'm just going to hold your sticks because I know I'm part of the package deal." He said that all the time, but Pascal wasn't just some player. He played well wherever I was with him. But it was awesome, a private jet came to pick us up in Montreal and flew us to Boston, where we met our new teammates. After the game in Boston, we flew to Pittsburgh and arrived at Mellon Arena the next day. I had a really good feeling about the whole thing from the beginning.

I had played against Mario Lemieux, but I don't know if he really knew who I was. We hadn't really talked before. I met him in the dressing room when I arrived in Pittsburgh. I remember seeing him that first time. He's tall. I wondered if I should go talk to him, my idol. He came to me, welcomed me to Pittsburgh, and told me this was a great opportunity for me. He told me to come to him if I needed anything. He was very nice and welcoming. Later in the playoffs as we got further, he was in the dressing room a lot. We'd have small chats. It was nice to have a legend like that in the room and just talking with him. But for me, it was always still like, wow, that's Mario Lemieux.

The Penguins had a young group of players who had never gone deep into the playoffs. It was a fun group of guys. There was Georges Laraque, who was this big guy who fought a lot, but he was as friendly as a teddy bear. On the bus and the plane, he'd sit right behind the coaches, and every time we walked through the aisle, you'd pass him and he'd hit you on your leg or shoulder. Everybody was like, no, Georges, don't do it, and he just kept laughing with his deep laugh and beating everybody up. Georges and I would hang out sometimes and go to the movies. I was by myself sometimes because Jana, who was then my fiancée, was studying and going to school back in Europe. Georges would invite me to the movies. For some reason, he liked paying for everything. Sometimes I'd go to pay for something and he'd already have paid for it. He just started laughing in his big laugh. I'd then go pay for dinner and that would also already be paid for and he'd be laughing again. I told him, "Well, I guess you don't want me paying for anything. It's not like you're that rich." He was fun to be around.

We also had Evgeni Malkin. He was such a talented Russian player. It was fun to watch him early in his career and see what he was already doing. We had a lot of fun on the power play with Sid, Malkin, and Ryan Malone at the front of the net and Sergei Gonchar or Kris Letang on the blue line. We had Marc-André Fleury in net and he was excellent. He was such a nice guy and a pleasure to be around. I was only there for four months, but we became like a family, especially with spending all that time together in a bubble during the playoffs. I enjoyed it. We had a lot of high-character guys.

And, of course, there was Sid. We became really close during that time. I sat beside him in the dressing room and we just clicked. He was such a professional from a young age. I had played against him, so I knew some things about him. He was a No. 1 pick and had all these expectations with being named captain right away. Everybody wanted to see how he was going to develop and handle all that. There are only a certain number of people who can deal with that type of pressure, and he was one of them. There's Jonathan Toews, Connor McDavid, those certain types, they can carry that. They're young, but they don't care. That's just how they are. Sid was like that. He was a really nice guy and professional, but he was also expecting everybody to put in 100 percent all the time. I think he saw that I was willing to do that.

We ended up creating a lot of chemistry on the ice, but that took some time. He was out of the lineup and then I was out of it with an injury. We only started playing more consistently together late in the season, just before the playoffs. We figured out we were able to work some give-and-gos and scored some goals. We were a good combo. I think he realized he could trust me to do what I do best and just work hard. I wasn't forcing it. It was just natural. I began producing more points. Obviously playing with Sid, the points do come easier. And as we went further and further in the playoffs, we were getting tighter. We were texting each other after games and becoming closer friends.

Michel Therrien was the coach of the Penguins then. When I got to Pittsburgh, guys were telling me at that first breakfast, "Hoss, you're going to see, he's like a madman," and this and that. I was like, "OK, let's see." And after the first week, I didn't see anything. I was like, "What are you guys talking about? You didn't experience Bob Hartley." They started asking me what I meant and began listening to my stories. Hartley was much harder to play for than Therrien. Therrien liked the way I worked and played me a ton. He was pretty quiet with me, so I had no idea what the other guys were talking about. I thought Therrien was going to be another Bob Hartley, but he was nothing like that. Compared to how tough Bob could be on younger players, Therrien was a walk in the park.

Entering the playoffs, I was optimistic, but you never know. In Ottawa, we had some really good seasons and were successful, but when it came to the playoffs, we just couldn't get past Toronto. We had won the Presidents' Trophy in 2003 and still lost in the conference finals. That was frustrating. People were saying we couldn't do anything in the playoffs. I had some good individual regular seasons, too, and didn't produce as much in the playoffs. With the Penguins, I got off to a slow start as well. I was creating a lot of chances but not finishing. I had 24 shots on goal in our first-round sweep of the Senators, but just one goal. I knew we were playing well and the production would come. I ended up with four assists in that series. I think we started realizing in that series we could be a pretty good team. We had so much quality throughout the lineup, a steady defense, and great goaltending. We gained confidence series after series.

At that point, I wasn't sure what I was going to do beyond that season. I was going to be a free agent. I was excited to be in Pittsburgh, but I wasn't thinking about re-signing there yet. The Penguins didn't know how I was going to perform, and I didn't know how I'd fit in with them. As a team, we didn't really have any expectations, but we kept on going deeper in the playoffs. I just tried to play my best. I think I did that. We didn't start talking about the possibility of being a Penguin and playing with Sid for another five years until after the season was over.

In the second round, we played the New York Rangers. They had swept the Thrashers when I was in Atlanta the year before. My brother, Marcel, had been with the Rangers the year before, but he had since been traded to the Coyotes. Jags was still with the Rangers. But during the second round, we started tearing it up. Sid and I were getting even more comfortable. We really starting to understand each other. I had four goals in that five-game series. In Game 5, I scored the game-winning goal in overtime. I remember we were getting really tired. We were going up against some quality players, including Jags. We faced him quite a bit in that series. In overtime, we started a rush in our zone, passed the puck, it came to me somehow, and it was one of those lucky shots that went between Henrik Lundqvist's legs. I closed my eyes, shot, and

Sid and I celebrating an overtime win against the Rangers in 2008
(Getty Images)

it went through his legs. I think I surprised him a little bit. Scoring that game-winning goal gave me a ton of confidence.

We played the Philadelphia Flyers in the Eastern Conference Final. Obviously that was a battle for Pennsylvania. Those were tough, tough games. We continued to play well, and our line was productive. We had a great overall feeling. I had four goals and five assists in that five-game series. I had some decent games against the Flyers in the playoffs during my career. Of course, I'd beat them again with the Blackhawks in the Stanley Cup Final a few years later. I just felt good in that rink for some reason. There was always a great atmosphere in that building and some crazy fans.

By then, my playoff beard was the longest it had ever been. I didn't cut it at all either. I wasn't trimming it, so it was just getting wild. I obviously like to be pretty clean and organized, but I was worried about breaking tradition, so I didn't touch my beard. After that season, I started keeping my playoff beard a bit more under control. But the overall feeling then, it was unbelievable reaching the Stanley Cup Final. I had never been that far before. You start realizing how close you are to your dream.

One of the things I'll never forget about all the Stanley Cup series, and especially the one against the Detroit Red Wings that season, was how much time I spent working on my sticks. It was even worse than when I was in Atlanta. My sticks came from a company called Mission. For whatever reason, the sticks would never arrive exactly the same. I'd have to tweak the curve a little bit. They'd come heavy, so I would have to shave them. I really spent so much time before the games on my sticks, like a crazy amount of time. I'd leave the morning skate early and start shaving them, so I could catch the bus and not be late. I wanted them to be perfect and they took a lot of time, but it paid off. I was happy with my play. I felt that if I took care of my sticks, they'd take care of me later. I can't remember if it was that Detroit series or the series before, but there was someone on the Flyers or Red Wings who must have known about my sticks. There were players who seemed to be stepping on my sticks on purpose in an attempt to break them. They did some damage to them and I'd have to spend time fixing the sticks again. I put in all this time and they'd do that; they definitely got in my kitchen.

Fast forward to the 2015 playoffs, and my sticks were already perfect when they arrived. I didn't have to worry about them at all. It was such a relief. My blade was thicker and the puck didn't bounce over it as much. I didn't have to worry about the weight. The curve was perfect and the same every time they arrived. I could just play and not worry about my stick. Before, I had to really shave the bottom to make it thinner and more flexible when I pushed down on it. The problem was it could easily break. So, I would shave the bottom and spray it black so it didn't seem as if it was shaved. But you also had to be careful because the referees were checking the curves back in the day. I had to be really keen on how I altered my stick and I learned how to cheat a little bit on the bottom of the stick. I'd have to shave a little bit off the bottom, so when the referee measured it, it had a better angle to touch the blade the whole way. They never actually took my stick, so I was pretty lucky. I think all my sticks were good at that point, though. But I did really have to strive to make them perfect. But back then, it was always on my mind about flying into a city and making sure I had enough time to make three perfect sticks.

Our initial problem against the Red Wings in that series was that we didn't treat them the same as we did our first three opponents in the playoffs. I think we showed them too much respect in the beginning of the finals. In the other series, we felt like, "We got these guys." But against the Red Wings, they had these big names and had already won a bunch of Stanley Cups. We started looking around for the first time, and before we knew it, we were already down 2–0 in the series. We were like, well, we better do something about it. We won Game 3 and Game 5 and got the series back to 3–2. In Game 6, we lost 3–2 in a close game in Pittsburgh. It took us a little bit to understand how to play them, and it was just too late by the time we figured it out.

Being at home for Game 6, we were especially disappointed to lose. We were thinking of what could happen in a Game 7 because there would have been so much pressure on them. That Game 6 loss was tough, too, because my parents were in town from Slovakia. We went to dinner after the game and talked about how close I had been to winning it all. But it was a great lesson overall for me. The Penguins fans were still really proud. You could feel that on the streets when they'd shake your hand. It was a young team and the Penguins were back in the finals and the city was alive again. It was obviously a good feeling, but everyone was still very disappointed.

THE NEXT DAY, we had our team meetings and everyone wanted to get home as soon as possible after the long season. We had a team dinner that night. I brought some Slovak alcohol, a full bottle of *slivovica*, that we had in our fridge. I think Gino, Letang, Fleury, and me, we all had a shot of it. Everyone was like, "Oh, my god." Your liver felt like it was getting paralyzed because it was such a strong alcohol. I told everyone they had to try it. Some went harder than others.

After that, Jana and I took a trip to the Bahamas for a week after the long season. I was disappointed because we had such a great run and fell short. I felt like I had my best years still in front of me and had just gotten a taste of the Stanley Cup

Final. I was driven to work hard and get there again the next season. I didn't know it, but Sid was actually in the Bahamas with a buddy too. We saw each other and had a couple drinks on the beach. I hadn't decided what I was going to do the next season. He obviously was surprised when I later signed with Detroit. He texted me something like, "You'll have to return to the nest next year." I think he meant I should go to Detroit for one season and then return to Pittsburgh. That next season with Detroit, we played Pittsburgh early in the season and Sid came over to the apartment for dinner. We had a good chat. We still have a good relationship. We've kept in touch ever since our first season together.

I'll also never forget the conversation I had with Mario as I was still deciding where to sign. Later that summer, I was driving back home in Slovakia and my cell phone rang. I knew it was an American number, so I picked it up. He said, "Hi, Marián, it's Mario Lemieux." All these things started running through my head. My idol was calling me. I started slowing down on the highway and pulled over into a gas station. From where I was parked, I had this amazing view of the Trenčín castle. I can still picture it. Mario told me they really wanted me back. Ritch had been negotiating with the Penguins and there was some distance between us. So, the Penguins had the big man with the hammer call me direct and try to make things move quicker. It was a smart move by them. But I told

Mario that I needed time to think about it. I thanked him for calling. I did really appreciate Mario calling me. It was a short conversation. I just didn't have an answer for him at that time. They were probably wondering why I hadn't decided yet. They were offering me five years and an opportunity to play with Sid and a young team. I told Mario I'd definitely think about it, would talk to my agent, and would let them know as soon as possible. They had a good team, they wanted me, and we had a great relationship, but for some reason, I envisioned something else. I decided to go with the Red Wings. The rest is history.

I wasn't worried about what people were going to say when I signed with Detroit. It was my decision and I had to stand by it. I was somewhat surprised how angry some of the reaction was in Pittsburgh. I had never pictured something like that happening. I thought I was there for four months and people would move on. When I saw videos of people burning my jersey, I was like, huh, it's bigger than I thought.

I DIDN'T PLAY with Sid for a long time, but he'll always be one of my favorite teammates. We just had something special on and off the ice. Sid was kind enough to share his memories about our time together with Scott.

Sidney Crosby

I knew a lot about [Marián] from watching him and then in Atlanta, but I had no idea that [trade] was gonna happen. I think I want to say that happened, like really late, like, right before the deadline. I was really pumped knowing that we were getting him.

I watched him when playing against Atlanta. He was just so good in every area. You could tell that he was really strong on the puck. I don't know how old he would have been when we got him. He seemed like he was dominant physically. I mean, even as a young guy in the league, I remember watching him and seeing clips and stuff, he was just strong. But at that point, I think he just started to pop off. He was powerful. I was really close with Colby Armstrong who went to Atlanta in that trade. When you're young and that stuff happens, it's kind of new. You never really do get used to it, but it was definitely new at that point. But we were really happy to get him and Pascal Dupuis. Those are some great guys to add to our team.

When Hossa came, I was hurt with my ankle, so we didn't get to play together. I remember being really excited to play with him and it ended up taking a little bit of time. I had a high-ankle sprain at the time and maybe a groin injury after that. But I'm pretty sure anybody could play well with Hoss. I mean, just the way he played a 200-foot game, the way he could do everything well. He could score. He could set up guys. He could hold onto the puck. He's so good defensively. I've never seen anybody get back on the backcheck...actually, him and Duper [Dupuis] are the only two guys I have ever seen get back that fast. It's kind of funny they came together.

I think obviously the more time you get together with someone, the better you learn from each other. But there's also guys where it kind of clicks right away, and he was one of those guys. He really liked to play a give-and-go game. He definitely could hold onto it if he needed to, but he liked moving the puck. He was really good down low holding on to it. I felt like we had some chemistry right away, which was great because we didn't have a lot of time to play together prior to the playoffs that year. It was easy to play with him.

I felt like right at the start of the playoffs we felt pretty good about our game. And definitely the playoffs, it's just different. It's a lot more pucks down low and a lot more battle-and-compete. I think everybody kind of raises their level. Hoss did that too. He was so strong, and then you throw in more meaningful games and more physical games; that's something that he could do easily just because of his size and the strength. So, yeah, he didn't shy away by any means.

I was a younger guy then, and for someone like him to come in, really easygoing, humble, took things really serious, worked really hard, he was a great example for me, and someone I looked up to. I felt really excited not to only play with him but to get to know him. I think we just clicked. We both like to compete and work hard and love to play. I think off the ice too. When someone comes in, it's a quick transition. You want to make them feel as comfortable as possible. He seemed really excited to be there, too, so I think it was just an exciting time. And we spent a lot of time together. Just having the opportunity to see him every day and hang out with him and pick his brain. I probably asked a few questions, but I really liked my time around him. He's a great guy.

I remember we got down in the [Detroit] series pretty quick. You're so excited to start this series, and all of a sudden, it's 2–0. But we had a lot of respect for that team, and the players that they had on it. I think looking back at the series, it was a lot closer of a series than it might have felt. We had so much respect for that team and all the guys and what they had done. They were kind of used to being there, and they had all the experience. It was something new for us, so it probably took us a little bit to really understand the position we were in and how to handle it.

I was a little [surprised Marián signed with Detroit], but I knew that there was a possibility that it could have been just a half year and him moving on. We had a lot of guys coming back, so I know we were pretty tight up against the cap. And I knew there was a lot of talk about a potential long-term deal and that sort of thing. So, I didn't really ask him a ton about it. I think we were both at the same spot on vacation, and that gave me a better idea. I knew that there were a few teams in the mix. He was trying to figure out whether he wanted to go long term or maybe do a short-term deal again and figure it out from there. I wouldn't say I was shocked, because I knew him pretty well and we had discussions. I knew there was a chance. It wasn't like he wasn't considering Pittsburgh and just saying that. He definitely considered it. But that's just kind of the decision he made, and I respected that.

I didn't try to recruit him too much. He'd spent some time there to get to know the guys. He knew we had a good group. We had a great run. So, I think for him to experience all that, he had a good idea of the guys who were returning. I didn't want to put that kind of pressure on him. Like I said, I know him fairly well, and it seemed like it was a pretty heavy process to have to make that decision.

It was weird [to play him in the finals the next season]. I mean, what are the chances of the same two teams playing each other back-to-back in the finals and Hoss having been on our team the year before? He had a great late chance to tie it in Game 6. We both kind of had a shot at it the year before when we lost. It was so random the way it worked out. That was tough to play [Detroit] two years in a row and the buildup, there's a lot of intensity and emotion that comes with that. But I have a lot of respect for him and I knew it couldn't have been easy.

I was happy [when he won the Cup with Chicago]. That's his third final in a row. And obviously, if we can't be there, I'm happy they are. We had lost to Montreal that year and we had a pretty good team. I think we ran out of gas a little bit with it being an Olympic year and having gone to the finals the previous two years. And I was thinking, he must be running on fumes, but seeing him out there and the way he was playing, I'm like, this is unbelievable. Like he was still flying, he looked strong, and to have to go through all that to play all that hockey, I was happy for him.

I think like anything, there are some people you meet in life, and you feel like you've known them for a long time, and he's just one of those guys. And even playing against him when he was in Atlanta, I wouldn't say I'm a big talker on the ice or buddy-buddy with guys, but I always liked watching him and playing against them. I liked the way he played. Even when he was in Atlanta, I think if I scored a nice goal or something like that, he'd be like, "Nice one," or something like that. There was a little bit of chatter here and there that I typically probably wouldn't have that often. For whatever reason, it kind of worked out that way.

I think the thing that stands out the most about him is his competitiveness and how he prepared. I think nowadays everybody trains pretty hard. It kind of comes with the territory. I think for him, seeing his dedication off the ice, the way he prepared and things like that, I think he was a pretty great example, especially for a guy who's on the younger side. I think the example he set was pretty unique.

RAY SHERO WAS the Penguins general manger when I was acquired and then when I departed. He also happened to be in Ottawa as an assistant general manager when the Senators drafted me. He also shared some thoughts with Scott.

Three

Ray Shero

I still remember the night before the '97 draft. Pierre Gauthier [Senators general manager], myself, Marshall Johnston [director of player personnel], Andre Savard [director of scouting], and Trevor Timmins [scouting coordinator] were at dinner. We were picking 12. Pierre's going through the list and what he thinks could happen. He turns to Marshall and goes, "Marshall, I could be wrong, but your guy could be there." We knew who he was talking about. Marshall looked at him, I'll never forget, and only Marshall could do this, he said, "Pierre, if he's fucking there, I'm telling you, I'm going to fall right out of my fucking chair, right out of my fucking seat." Sure enough, he was there. I don't know if Marshall fell out of his seat, but it was close. It was a heck of a pick. Those guys deserve a lot of credit. It was great to see.

[Marián's] brother was a couple years younger, but Marcel used to hang around the locker room. I think this was Marián's rookie year, before we sent him back to Portland. Marcel was around. The trainers would be like, "Gee, whiz, fucking Hossas. Marián's brother keeps stealing tape." I'm like, Jesus Christ, I'm not going to track down the brother for tape. Well, back then we're with Ottawa, so I'm like, "How much tape did he take?" (laughing)

I'll never forget the first game [after acquiring Marián] was in Boston. The hype was, you know, the Penguins add Marián Hossa. I was in Ottawa when he was at the Memorial Cup and he tore his

53

ACL. I remember that quite vividly and going through that. Then in the second period in his first game with Pittsburgh, he got hit by someone at the blue line and went down holding his knee. We lost 5–1. He's getting helped off the ice, and I swear to God, I'm in the press box in Boston on the ninth floor, and I looked at my assistant GM Chuck Fletcher and he looks at me, and I say, "I think I'm going to fucking throw up." And he goes, well, maybe it's not that bad. I just looked at Chuck and said, "Fuck we just gave up a hell of a lot for Pascal Dupuis." It had to be the longest 10, 15, 20 minutes, whatever it was, waiting for the medical trainer to text me. It was one of the best texts I ever got. Our trainer texted me and said Boston's doctor looked at him, we've looked at him, it might be one or two weeks, it might be two to four weeks, something like that. I'm like, I don't give a fuck, as long as you don't say it's season-ending or something. So that was his first game.

It took him a little time to really sync with the team and in the playoffs. I still remember, when he came back, he might have played 10, 12 games for us, but I remember we're playing someone near the end of the season. This was after the second period. It might have been against the Rangers, a nationally televised game. I remember walking down after the period to grab a coffee or something in the old press box in Pittsburgh. I remember some guy yelling at me, some Pittsburgh fan, "Hey, Shero, I thought you were getting some fucking winger for Crosby. This guy sucks." I'm like, Jesus Christ, I'll get Colby Armstrong back. I mean, oh boy.

It's funny, he came back, played the 11, 12 games with us at the end of the season, and then the playoffs were just another level for him. It's such a great thing and he's obviously a Hall of Famer and all that stuff, but he's got to be one of the most underrated players of all time. It's crazy. And how good this guy was, defensively, killing penalties. He was so good. I think it was in the second round we beat the Rangers at home in overtime. I think it was Game 5, and Marián scored the game-winner in overtime. That was such a great feeling and great feeling for him, I'm sure. He had a hell of a playoff run for us. Against Detroit, he played great. Those Detroit teams were so great. You can't blame him after playing them for six games. "How about trying that for one year?" We offered him five years, $7 million a year. It wasn't about the money. It wasn't a 12-year deal or something. It was just a one-year deal.

I still remember we beat them in the Final obviously the next year. I sent him an email a few days or weeks after and told him how much I respected him and, going back a year ago, the decision he made and never regretting it and it was from his heart and it wasn't about the money. I got a really nice email from him back saying, holy cow, so nice to hear from you and congratulations on the Cup, how well you guys played after the trade deadline, and you should get GM of the year or something. I'm laughing. It was one of those classy things. I ran into him at a shopping mall in downtown Chicago when I was with Jersey or someone and we were shooting the shit. He had been 0 for 2 with Cups before, but at this point, he had won three with

Chicago. I said to him, you're now leading 3–2. There's now a positive side. It couldn't happen to a better guy. I respected that decision he made with me in Pittsburgh. He was up front and honest with me and he did it from his heart and head. It all worked out and couldn't have happened to a better guy.

Four

As tradition demanded, I stood in line with the rest of my Penguins teammates and shook hands with the Detroit Red Wings after losing to them in the Stanley Cup Final. I was disappointed. We were so close. At the end of the line was Red Wings coach Mike Babcock. We shook hands, and he said, "Come to Detroit next year. We really want you." I didn't know what to say. I just said, "Congratulations," and walked away.

I woke up the next morning and began thinking about it more. Why did he say that then? It was unexpected. I put it away, but it came back to me as I was training that summer. I obviously had a choice to make. I was going to sign somewhere. The idea that Mike Babcock really wanted me was going through my mind. But why would I want to leave this

Pittsburgh team? They also wanted me. They had a good group. Sid and I had a great relationship.

But for some reason, I had this thought that I needed to go to the Red Wings and learn something more. I saw how Pavel Datsyuk played, Henrik Zetterberg, Chris Chelios, and Nick Lidström. They had all these future Hall of Famers and such a successful team. Also, learning the work ethic needed from guys like Chris Draper would be a great lesson. I knew on the one hand it might be crazy to leave Pittsburgh and sign with Detroit, but I also thought I could gain something being in that dressing room and on the ice with all those great players. I sought to learn from the best of the best, players who had won Stanley Cups. I wanted what they had. So, I signed with the Detroit Red Wings on a one-year, $7.4 million deal.

How that contract came about is a story in itself. And to tell that story, I asked my agent Ritch Winter and then Red Wings general manager Ken Holland to join me on a call and talk about how we actually came to finalize that deal in the summer of 2008.

Here's our conversation:

Ritch Winter: Marián and I had met in Atlanta in his last year during the 2007–08 season. We started talking about his future, and I insisted we set some goals based on Marián's vision for the success he wanted to see in the rear-view mirror of his career once they locked the dressing room door behind him. It's how we started targeting Detroit to some degree. Because Marián saw holes in his NHL experience that, once he thought about it, needed to be addressed if he was going to become the best of which he was capable. He knew he needed to experience things that eluded him to that point in his career. Team success and learning from a group of players who had done what he wanted most, to win that last game of the season at the NHL level.

Marián Hossa: I remember we were in Atlanta at the Westin. Obviously I had a lot of success getting lots of points and lots of goals, but I wanted the team success. We were searching for the teams with quality. Maybe I could pick up something from future Hall of Famers. Detroit was definitely one of those teams. I didn't know I was going to get traded to Pittsburgh at that time before the deadline, but we started searching for certain teams with quality players I could play with for a long time, or ones who had a good chance to win a Stanley Cup. I told Ritch, these are the teams I want to go to because I want to win the Stanley Cup. That was the key for us.

Ken might not know this. But when the Red Wings beat us in the Stanley Cup Final the season before, we were shaking hands after the game, and Mike Babcock was at the end of the line. I said, congratulations and shook his hand. He just held it for one second and said, "Come to Detroit." I'm thinking about this in the dressing room afterward. Obviously I'm disappointed in my mind, but why would somebody who just won the Stanley Cup tell me this right after? I'm like, what the hell is wrong with him?

Ken Holland: (laughing) I never heard that before. That's the first time I heard that.

Winter: I had one of the more unusual meetings I've ever had after that Stanley Cup Final. I went up to the draft and met with Chuck Fletcher and Ray Shero, who were assistant GM and GM of the Penguins at the time. They offered Marián five years times $7.5 million. Their pitch was, look, that's the same term as Sidney Crosby, so if Sid leaves, you can leave. They thought for sure there was no way anybody would say no to that deal. Sidney Crosby, same term, $7.5 million? Like, there's not a chance. Well, I had done the analytics and we looked at it pretty carefully, and despite the fact that the Red Wings would lose to them the next year, if they had put $7.5 million extra into forwards, they may not have been able to sign Kris Letang, and our analytics said that probably wasn't going to be a Stanley Cup champion or as good as they would have been without signing another defenseman. They were actually in some ways better *without* Marián because they were able to shore up their back end. So, we made that decision.

Marián, I don't know what was going on in your head at that time, but I can tell you, when I walked into that room and said, "No, thank you" to Chuck and Ray, they never saw that one coming. Ultimately, since it's a team game, we simply helped them do the right thing for the Pens, no matter how attractive it was to sign Marián.

Hossa: After we lost in the Final, obviously Pittsburgh offered me a great term in the five-year deal and great money to play with a young superstar in Sid. For some reason, when I look back, I don't know what I was thinking. Like, what the hell was I thinking? But for some reason, I had that drive to go to Detroit because I saw the huge names there. I thought I could learn something from them, even for the one year. I knew I could have a good chance to win, but that wasn't guaranteed. I knew I could go far and learn from those guys to be a better hockey player, how to handle myself on and off the ice. Those guys were great examples. I didn't care about the long term. I just cared about going to a good team and maybe learning something from those guys.

Ken had so much success already as a GM and managing that team. He had a great coaching staff. Babcock was focused so much on the team. I saw a great opportunity. I knew that it was most likely going to be a small chance for me re-signing with Detroit after the one season, but I didn't care. I wanted to at least one year be a Red Wing for some reason, and that was my goal. Because there were other really good opportunities—Pittsburgh, or there was a crazy deal from Edmonton.

Winter: I think about it more now as I've gotten to know you better. I think the decision was largely based on the fact that you felt like you would be a better player being with Nick Lidström, Pavel Datsyuk, Henrik Zetterberg, and Chris Chelios. That was the most interesting thing about it. Very few athletes give up an offer like Edmonton's. We thought we could have got to $80, maybe $80 million-plus. I thought it was incredible that Marián drilled down and decided he wanted to be a better player. You didn't want to leave the game missing something like this. Not many players make a goal that could cost them $70 million-plus, but Marián was focused and knew what he wanted from the game. It was more about potential and achievement than it was money.

I am always telling players that there are two things in every NHL standard player contract—money and opportunity. I always push players to chase opportunity first and foremost, because the money will follow. Always! But, walking away from $70 million was a gutsy call few players would make. Few, if any agents, would give a second thought to the money. But Marián knew that his potential as a player would never be fulfilled if he was to join the Oilers at that point. He may have lost $10 to $15 million in earnings, but, in retrospect, it seems like a small investment, because he would have entered the Hockey Hall of Fame without the Cups he won in Chicago, because of the experience he brought to the kids there, based in large part on what he learned in Detroit. It was telling that Marián chose to have Nick Lidström present him his plaque at the HHOF induction ceremony. Nick was everything Marián wanted to be as an athlete and the two are, in my view, among the best fathers, husbands, and teammates their families and teams would ever have. They have had that in common from the get-go.

Before we even talked to Ken, we knew that they would probably not be able to sign you long term because of the contract with Henrik Zetterberg coming up, which Ken was going to make a focus. A lot of people in your situation, players are just looking for the long-term money and security. We recognized very early on that Detroit was probably not going to provide you with a long-term opportunity, but it was going to provide you more of a chance to play as part of the big red machine and play with those guys.

Holland: Don Waddell, who was the general manager of Atlanta, had been my assistant general manager in Detroit previously. At the trade deadline that year, I did have a couple of conversations with Don about trying to acquire Marián. I don't remember if it was the price or what, but it kind of went bye-bye, and then I saw Marián got traded to Pittsburgh. As a manager, you're always looking one and two years out. You know who's going to be free this summer, but who's also going to be free next summer. From afar, I thought, wouldn't it be nice to get Marián to be part of the Detroit Red Wings? I explored it at the trade deadline and Marián went to Pittsburgh, and I thought well, that's over, he's going to a good team and they've added a good player.

So now, July 1 is free agency. Two weeks earlier, we had beaten Pittsburgh. We had won the Stanley Cup. It's the night before free agency, it's June the 30th. We were preparing. We had a team scouts' meeting. We wanted to make some little additions to our team. We were going to try to win the Cup back-to-back. I remember reading online about how Marián had turned down a big-money deal in Pittsburgh and then there's rumblings that there was a big-money and long-term offer from Edmonton. So you know, I don't think there's a chance Hossa is coming to Detroit, so we're focused in on some other guys.

So I go to bed on June 30th. I wake up in the morning and I'm going to head down to the office for free agency. I leave my house and I go to a gas station. I'm getting gas and I'm sitting at the pump. There's a little sign there: no cell phones. But my phone is ringing in my pocket. I pulled my phone out, so the attendant can't see it. I can see it says Ritch Winter, but I stuff the phone back in my pocket. I go, I'll get Ritch later. About two minutes later, Ritch calls me back again. I'm thinking to myself, why is he calling me twice? Now I better answer. I sort of slide down below the car, so that guy sitting in the window can't see me. I get down below the car, and I put the phone by my ear, and I said, "Hi Ritch, I'm in a gas station, I can't talk."

Winter: I said, "Marián asked me to call you, Ken. He's very interested in coming to Detroit."

Holland: I said, "I don't have the kind of money that I hear you are talking about online."

Winter: I said, "Well, he's asked me to talk to you about a one-year deal."

Holland: I said, "A one-year deal? I'm all in. I can't talk now. I can't talk right now. I'm at a gas station and there's a guy by the window looking. I'm gonna drive down to the rink and I'll call you. I'll call you in 45 minutes." So I hung up the phone, and my heart was pounding for the next half hour thinking what kind of wonderful present has Ritch Winter got for the Red Wings.

Winter: I think we talked a little bit and you asked me what I was thinking on a one-year deal.

Holland: I said, "I can't afford Marián. You've got multi-million-dollar, multi-year offers. I don't have that kind of cap space."

Winter: I said, "No, no, Ken, hold on, we're willing to do a one-year deal."

Holland: OK, so you've got my attention. I think you said to me, how about a one-year deal at like $8.5. I had the cap space for that. Zetterberg was making around $2.75 for one more year, and I think Valtteri Filppula had another year. So I had all the players with the numbers low, and I had cap space for one year. I said, "Ritch, I got lots of cap space on a one-year deal. I'm interested in a one-year deal, $8 million."

Hossa: If the money was important, I would be in Edmonton and probably pretty miserable, because at that time Edmonton was a team rebuilding and they didn't have as many great players to play with. There would have been a great opportunity to play high-level minutes, but I was ready at my peak to play the best hockey and I needed somebody to play with me. We were looking also at Chicago, but Chicago had signed Brian Campbell to a long-term deal and their salary cap was already full. Detroit was the option.

Winter: I called Marián to confirm. Marián said, yeah, the money wasn't that important. I don't know if he would have said yes to $7 million. Six million, he might have said, no. But Marián was like, that sounds good. I called you back.

Holland: I said, "If you're serious, I gotta make one call. I want to call Nick Lidström out of respect. He's making $7.5. He's the captain and he's taking the hometown discount. I just want to call him and give him a heads up that I'm going to bring in somebody that's making more money. So, just give me 15 minutes to try to track him down and I'll get back to you."

Winter: I called Marián to say what you're doing. "It's gonna take a bit of time, but we have a deal." Marián says to me, "Well, no, no, just phone him back, tell him I'll take $7.4, I don't want to bother Nick on vacation." So I pick up the phone and I recall sort of playing with you a little bit, and saying, "Well, you know, I talked to Marián, and we got a counteroffer, Ken, because he's been thinking about it."

Holland: My heart sank when you said a counteroffer. I thought it was going up.

Winter: "Marián's asked me to offer you similar term, but he only wants $7.4 because he doesn't want you to bother Nick."

Holland: Marián Hossa, one year at $7.4? I said, "Done. I'm not even going to call Nick. Ritch, we got a deal." We hung up the phone, and I go running into Jimmy Nill's office, my assistant general manager. I'm floating on air. The Stanley Cup champions have added Marián Hossa to the team. It's six Christmases packed into one. I close the door, and I said to Jimmy, "You will never believe what happened, we just added Marián Hossa." He said, "Marián Hossa? Ken, how many millions, how many years did you pay him?" I said, "Jimmy, it's one year, it's $7.4." Jimmy said, "Doesn't the rumor mill say he's been offered long-term, big-money deals?" I said, "Jimmy,

I'm as confused as you are, but I'm not saying no, we've gotten Marián Hossa."

So we sit down in Jimmy Nill's office, the two of us, and we're excited and the clock goes by as we wait for the contract. A half hour turns into an hour turns into an hour and a half.

Winter: I told you to fax the contract to some number Marián had given me for some guy who had a fax machine down the road from him.

Hossa: Probably, I can't remember.

Winter: So Ken's waiting for us to get back to them.

Holland: We're sitting there and I hear no response. So now Jimmy and I are starting to second guess it. Marián's coming to his senses. He's not coming to Detroit. He's realized that there's too many millions out there for too many years. We've lost him. We've lost him. He's not coming. So now, Jimmy and I are starting to panic. I'm getting nervous. We're gonna lose Marián. So I said to Jimmy, "I got an idea. I want to call Ritch, and let's see if we can get Marián on a Detroit radio station interview, and once he goes on the radio station for the interview, then we know we've got him."

I said to you, "Ritch, would Marián mind going on a Detroit radio station this afternoon at 3 p.m., the fans would like to hear from Marián. All the fans like Marián." Ritch hangs up. Ritch calls me back and says, "Sure, yeah, he'll go on the radio station." Now I'm sitting there. We're nervous wrecks, Jimmy and I. We've got Marián Hossa, we've got Marián Hossa. We've lost Marián Hossa, we've lost Marián Hossa. Once Marián went on the Red Wings radio station at 3 p.m.—he did call in, you did go on to radio, they interviewed him and talked about coming to join the Red Wings—I was sky high because I knew it was now official. I wasn't quite as worried about the faxed contract. I knew it was official. I knew we had a deal, one year and $7.4 to the Stanley Cup champions. We're adding Marián, a great, great player to our team. Marián Hossa, what an offseason.

Winter: You got to keep in mind, Jim Nill and I grew up near each other. He and I went to high school together. We dated the same girls. I would think Jim would say at some point, look, I know Ritch, I think you can trust him. But you just couldn't believe it. I am still upset by the fact that I've never gotten a Christmas card. All I've delivered to Ken is Marián Hossa and Dominik Hašek. The funny thing is every conversation I had with Ken about a big-money player, we kept giving money back. He wants to offer $8 million and Marián wants $7.4. That follows on the heels of two years earlier when Hašek had come back at $6 million. He pulled his groin and everybody was beating him up. So I call Ken at that time, and say, "Hey, Dom feels bad about the groin, he didn't come back to be on the injured reserve, so he'd like to give half his salary back." So not only do I deliver the superstars, but for some reason, they want to keep giving the money back. It's crazy.

Holland: I can't seem to make that happen anymore. Ritch, you got to get some more players.

Hossa: When I look back, I don't know what I was thinking. But that was there in my mind and I just tried to follow my vision. I didn't really look left or right. Even my father asked me, can you explain to me what just happened? Five-year deal with long-term security, playing with the great players in Pittsburgh, and you signed a one-year deal with the Red Wings? Nobody saw that coming. I didn't talk to my parents about that. I talked to Ritch and basically I had my vision in my mind, and that's what happened. I saw something and I went there.

Some would probably say that karma got me in the end, with our loss to the Penguins in the Final that next season. Obviously we wanted to win so bad and I wanted to win so bad, and it is still frustrating when I look back. We lost and we were so close. You can't get any closer, with Game 7 and one goal at the end. But I believe if I wasn't there that year, I wouldn't have learned how to play a proper 200-foot game. Playing with Pavel Datsyuk, he made the game so easy for me. I'd stay on the ice with Pavel quite a bit and we were stealing pucks from each other. I picked up lots of things from him. When I left the Red Wings, I was a way better player than before. That year gave me so much. Even though we lost, I learned quite a bit from that loss, because that was devastating. But I think that made me stronger mentally that year. When I signed with the Blackhawks, I was more ready for certain situations in the playoffs mentally.

Holland: It's interesting what Marián said about his experience playing with Z and Pav, because I don't know how many times after Marián left Detroit and went to Chicago I told my staff how good of a player Marián was, a 200-foot player. But I think when we acquired Marián, I was thinking of an offensive guy that was going to come and produce offense and score goals, and I didn't think about his defensive part of the game. And watching him, and maybe I didn't pay enough attention, but certainly now and hearing Marián talk about the impact of that, watching Pav, playing with Pav, playing with Z, and the way that we played the game, and then watching you in Chicago, again, I said many, many times, holy cow is Marián ever a good 200-foot player. The way you would track people and backchecked and stole pucks.

Winter: Coach John Wooden, who is I think the greatest coach ever, said success is the satisfaction you get from knowing you did the best to which you're capable. In my mind, Marián is one of the few guys I've worked with who wanted to be the best they could be. I really looked at this as him making a decision that was going to give himself every opportunity to be the best he could be. That's sort of why we decided on Detroit, and it wasn't like there was another option. I remember Cheli phoned me and said, "What are you guys doing? You're coming here to win the Cup? Like, you know, stuff happens in a one-year deal, there's no guarantee, guys get injured." I said, "No, he'd like to win the Cup, but he's really coming here to become a better player." Cheli thought that was pretty cool.

Hossa: During that next season, I think it was February, we were doing good and it was before the playoffs, and Ken called me into his office. You had your screen locked down and when I came over, you opened it up for me. You said, "These are the guys I need to sign. I really want you, but if you want to stay here, this the only cap room we got for this many years." So we had talked about this, and I kind of listened and I tried to analyze in my mind the possibilities, and obviously we went over it a couple times back and forth.

I knew at that time obviously Zetterberg was the No. 1 choice for the Red Wings, you know, future captain and a great player. I knew Johan Franzén was the second choice because he was playing really well at the time. Obviously there were a big number of Swedes. I knew that maybe I'd be No. 3 at the time, even though Datsyuk and I were playing really well and we were scoring goals and winning games and everything was really nice. But I kind of knew, most likely, these guys are going to go ahead of me. I wasn't going to be naïve. I took a discount and could have gone somewhere else, but I wanted to be a Red Wing for at least one year. If there's a chance to re-sign, great, but if not, I knew I would have to probably look somewhere else. So, that's what happened.

We lost in the Final. I talked to Babcock when we had the meetings, and obviously Babcock was disappointed, like me. We were flat at the end in the last game against Pittsburgh. Babcock said, "Good season, Hoss, but we'll see what's going to happen." I just kind of sensed it from him. He was different from the beginning from when he wanted me to be with the Red Wings. I wasn't sure if he really wanted me there anymore. That kind of got me thinking, maybe I should go somewhere else.

Holland: Wow.... As it turned out, we went to Zetterberg right off the bat, and I got Zetterberg done with a 13-year deal. You and I engaged a little bit in February, and then I didn't sense enough traction. So then I went to Franzén and got him done with an 11-year deal. We ended up losing in the Final, and I went to Mr. Ilitch [Red Wings owner], and told him I'd like to try to keep Marián Hossa in a Red Wings uniform, but I'm gonna have to get a long-term deal because it's got to be a low cap number. It's gonna be a lot of years, 13 years at $4.5. It was around $52-$53 million. As it turned out, you got $10 million more, you got it structured differently, but certainly my goal was to keep all three of you in a Red Wing uniform.

So Ritch came to me, I think shortly after we lost the Pittsburgh series. We had played Chicago and we beat them in five games, but you could tell they were on the move. They had Jonathan Toews and Patrick Kane and a good young team. Then, you asked me for permission prior to July 1.

Winter: I believe I said, "Ken, we'll do the one-year deal, we'll give you a $600,000 haircut, but the minute your season's over, we'd like to talk to other teams."

Holland: Yes, that's correct.

Winter: I wanted permission because I know Marián pretty well. He's a very studied guy. He likes to take his time. I thought, OK, if we're doing this crazy thing and turning down $80 to $100 million, I, at least, want the opportunity to speak to other teams before July 1. We don't know how much time we're gonna have. You could go out in the first round, second round. So that's when I started engaging Chicago. And quite frankly, the funniest thing about that is, Chicago was the place that we looked at and the analytics said, you add Marián's expected production to what they have and the growth that is likely to come from within, we didn't say that's a Stanley Cup winner, but we said, look, that's a team that has a very high probability of being in the final four on a regular basis for a long time. We picked that destination.

Holland: I feel very, very fortunate that we got Marián to play for the Red Wings for a year. Marián said he learned a lot, but I think it was great for the Detroit Red Wings to have Marián there for a year. We got to the finals again. We were up three games to two in the finals against Pittsburgh, and they found a way to win Games 6 and 7. And I'm not sure if we go to the finals the second year again without Marián. Marián came in and gave us that energy. When we won the cup in 2008–09, we brought in Dallas Drake, someone who had never won the Cup before, and the guys wanted Dallas Drake to experience that. Marián brought that energy and was a professional and helped us get back to the finals two consecutive years. We just ran out of gas a little bit at the end. So, it was a win-win. Marián used the opportunity and went on to Chicago, and what a crew you had in Chicago, winning three Stanley Cups. Everything you helped that team accomplish, and you had an incredible, incredible career. And I feel fortunate that you made a decision to be in Detroit for a year.

Winter: I think the message for all this is, every time you chase the money, I've never found chasing the money to lead to too much value for a player in the end. If Marián Hossa has X million dollars in the bank or X-point five, it doesn't change his life because X is going to be very large. And I think it's interesting, I've always believed if you chase opportunity, money will always be sufficient. But if you chase money, the opportunity might be depressing, and we've seen that.

Holland: I'm with you, 100 percent. That's what I try to sell. I reflect back on the Detroit days and Marián, Dominik Hašek, Zed, what made that group special was they all sacrificed with the ice time, they sacrificed at the negotiating table. And certainly it's a different time now, I don't want to judge, but I think you should chase happiness. We all make enough money in this industry, but do you like to go to work every day? Do you like to play with your teammates? Do you have a chance to win? Do you like where you live? It's way better if you go to work every day, to the rink every day, and you feel happy about where you're at in life.

Winter: I think it's really important to Marián. Just ask players like James Neal. He destroyed his career by pushing for a bit more from Calgary over Las Vegas. I have never seen a player chase and select opportunity and regret it. Not Marián. Not Michal Rozsíval. Not Martin Straka. Definitely not Dominik Hašek. Their decisions would define them.

Holland: I tip my cap to Marián. Ritch, you sat down with Marián in Atlanta. It was a tough go there, an expansion team. I think they made the playoffs once in 11 years, and you and Marián mapped out a plan that identified some teams that Marián would like to go to because winning was more important than goals and assists, team statistics, and making

Ritch holding the Stanley Cup at my Hockey Hall of Fame dinner

money. You obviously went to Pittsburgh, and Marián says he shook his head a few times why he didn't take the five-year deal with Pittsburgh, but he went to Detroit, went to Chicago. And certainly when you made the decision to come to Detroit, you left lots of money, lots of term, lots of security, you bet on yourself, but you made the decisions for the right reasons. And as it turns out, all those right reasons are probably a factor why you ended up in Chicago with Toews and Kane, won the Stanley Cups. You made the decisions in your career for the right reasons and everything else takes care of itself.

Winter: I don't know if you remember this, Marián, I always like to talk about some big crazy goal, you know. I recall you saying, "Well, maybe we should put down like three Stanley Cups, right?"

Hossa: My goal, my dream was to win one Stanley Cup. We'd see what would happen next, but the goal was one Cup. I wanted to experience that when I played hockey because I wanted to get that trophy and put my name on it and that would be a dream come true. That's why I played the game. And obviously, that was my goal. If we win an extra one, that would be a bonus, but, you know, we never thought there would be something like three Stanley Cups.

Holland: You know what? Ritch, when I was in that gas station and the phone rang the first time and I actually stuffed the phone back in my pocket because I saw the guy looking and there was a big sign about no cell phone use—if you had said to yourself, you know what, forget Ken Holland, he didn't even pick up, I'm going to go elsewhere, Marián would never have been a Red Wing. But two minutes later, you called back. I looked at it again and thought boy, is Ritch persistent, I better see what he's up to. And actually the call that time led Marián to becoming a Red Wing. So, thanks for your persistence.

Winter: Thanks, at least on this one occasion, for breaking Michigan state law, because it worked out pretty well.

Five

If you asked me to word associate my one season with the Detroit Red Wings, most of my answers probably wouldn't come as a surprise to you. I'd give you words like winners, legends, professionals, and so on. But how about track suits and red wine? You wouldn't expect those, would you? From the moment I stepped on the plane with that Detroit team, I knew I was joining a different group, and track suits and red wine had something to do with that.

So, first, let me explain the track suits. My experience up until Detroit was getting on team planes while wearing my suit, wearing it throughout the trip, and then coming home in that same suit. Playing in Ottawa, Pittsburgh, and Atlanta, most of our flights were pretty short. Because Detroit was centrally located and often had to travel longer distances being in the Western Conference, those players were on their planes for much longer. To remain comfortable on those long flights, the players would wear their dress clothes onto the flights and then change into something different. They'd then change back before departing. I didn't know this the first time. But that second time, I brought along my track suit and changed into it just like everyone else.

As for the red wine, that was the go-to drink for a lot of those players. I didn't know where to sit on the place at first. I sometimes sat with Tomáš Kopecký or Jiří Hudler, a Czech guy. Near him, there were guys playing cards. Sometimes I sat there with them. They would order red wine all the time. I began doing it too. I enjoyed having red wine with that group. You never overdid it, but it was nice to have a glass or two. Nick Lidström and Chris Chelios, two Norris Trophy winners and legends, were sitting back there with Tomas Holmström at the card table. That was really cool to be a part of. On the long flights, we'd talk a lot, play cards, and have a couple glasses of red. I'd just sit back, listen to all their stories, and laugh.

OK, something about Mike Babcock. I have to say, he was the best coach I played for in terms of preparing his team for the opponent. He was all about the details, and I liked that. He was really focused on his job, and that's why he was so successful at what he did. He also could be sarcastic at times. Those sarcastic comments could be draining on his players.

Guys usually get tired of playing for a coach like that after a few years. I believe that's why he was later fired in Detroit. I only played for Babs for a year and I learned a lot, but I was also glad to have someone new behind the bench the following season.

Cheli and Mike Babcock didn't have the best of relationships, as you may know. They'd go at after each other sometimes. Cheli wouldn't be playing as much as he liked and he'd give it to Babcock, and Babcock would give it back to him. I remember us landing from somewhere in the middle of the night, and everyone was changing back into their suits. But Cheli didn't change. He didn't bother. He just left the plane with whatever he had on. I was like, wow, what a legend. He didn't give a shit. He did his own thing, and that's why people loved him.

Before coming to Detroit, I had always heard these tall tales about Chris Chelios. You heard about how he was always in top shape and how hard he worked. I was looking forward to seeing him do those things in person. He wasn't playing a lot and would be a healthy scratch. I was hurt one time and was walking through the locker room during a game and saw a trainer pulling a stationary bike into the sauna. I asked what he was doing. He said, "Oh, Cheli does this all the time." He'd ride the bike in the sauna and watch the game. I watched him and he'd be sweating like crazy. Later on while I was still hurt,

I decided to give the same routine a try. I was sweating badly and I couldn't breathe. It was such a different experience. It was a good experience, too, but I'd never do it again.

I had known Jiří a little bit before I arrived in Detroit, but we got real close there. He was a smaller player, but he was really talented. He was an excellent passer. I spent a lot of time with him that season. Jana, who was still my fiancée then, wouldn't always be there because she was in university, so I'd be home alone and he was mostly alone too. We'd go to breakfast or dinner. We got together quite a bit that year. I'd hang out also with Kopecký, but his family was there, so Kopy would usually stay home with his two little kids after long trips.

There was this one time Jiří and I went to a sushi place for dinner. There was this green stuff, wasabi, a sauce which goes on the sushi. Some girl Jiří knew was sitting at the bar alone, so he invited her to join us. She told us she had never eaten at a sushi place before. I could just see Jiří's eyes spark. She asked us to explain what wasabi was. Jiří was the type of guy who liked to joke around. So he told her wasabi was like an appetizer. I was thinking to myself, what is this guy doing? I was kicking him under the table, but he was signaling to me not to worry. He grabs a little ball of wasabi and puts it into her mouth. Two seconds later, she starts spitting it all out and running to the bathroom. He was laughing like crazy. I was like, oh my god, what are you doing? She came back, packed her bag and left, and he just kept laughing. I have to say it was pretty funny, but it was also funny when she gave him the finger and left.

Kopy, I knew somewhat from back home. He's originally from the town over from me in Slovakia, but he played in Trenčín. He was the same age as my brother and Marián Gáborík. We also got to know each other better in Detroit. He signed with the Blackhawks that next season too. In Detroit, he took me around and showed me the city and would invite me out for dinners. I'd go to his house and spend time with him and his family. We became closer throughout our three seasons together and still see each other quite a bit. We'd drive together to and from the airport in Detroit. On the way there, we'd talk a lot about home. On the way back, we'd discuss the game. Our thing also became ordering two *doppios* before going to games. We had our double espressos from Starbucks. When I got to Detroit, I didn't drink much coffee, but I began trying it more. After that, I kept going with it.

That whole season went pretty well for me and the team. I scored 40 goals that season. Through the 2021–22 season, I believe I am the last player to score 40 goals in a season for the Red Wings. I thought I played well, but I obviously had some really talented players around me too. You'll hear plenty about me playing with Pavel Datsyuk in the next chapter. I learned so much from him. He was a special player.

There were so many great players on that team. I got to play some with Henrik Zetterberg. He was a world-class centerman. There was a great group of Swedish players on

I learned so much playing in Detroit with great players like Nicklas Lidström and Pavel Datsyuk *(Getty Images)*

that team. Having played one season in Sweden, I got to talk to them about that. It was really a great group of guys and I really enjoyed my time with them.

That season we played the Blackhawks at Wrigley Field in the Winter Classic. That's something I'll never forget. The atmosphere was amazing. My parents and Jana came in for the game. Despite the cold, I played well. I had three assists in the win. Because it was Chicago, Kenny Holland wanted Cheli playing in the game. He hadn't been playing much. So Cheli dressed for the game, but Babcock also decided to dress seven defensemen and just play him a few minutes. Babs was showing everyone who the bench boss was. Cheli sat on the bench for most of the game. Late in the game, Babcock told him to get on the ice, and Cheli told him something like, fuck off. He just didn't give a shit, and I don't blame him.

Being traded to Pittsburgh the season before, I had felt some personal pressure, but there was more of it in Detroit. The Penguins were a young team and hadn't won a Cup yet. The Red Wings were an experienced team that had just won a Cup. The expectation was to win another one and repeat. Plus, I was the big addition that offseason. No one else was coming. So, I did feel the additional pressure.

What are the chances of the same two teams meeting in the Stanley Cup Final two years in a row? It was just my luck. And now I was playing for the other team. I knew my hands were going to be tight entering the series. I just told myself to try to focus and play them as if they were any other opponent.

As a team, we played well the first two games and got out to a 2–0 advantage. The Penguins kept fighting. We had a chance to close them out in Game 6 in Pittsburgh. The game was so tough. I remember I just didn't have it that night. I felt like it was tough to skate, my legs were dragging. I don't know what happened. I don't know if it was the pressure or the atmosphere there, but it felt like something was getting to me. We ended up losing that game. We flew back to Detroit late that night. I remember thinking how close I was to being a champion, just one win away.

I woke up early the day of Game 7 and went to the balcony of the penthouse I rented in the Royal Oak area. I looked around and told myself, this could be the day I've dreamed about my entire life. I was one win away. I dressed and drove to the old Joe Louis Arena for the morning skate.

In Game 7, we had chances to win again. It was all down to the wire. We struggled to score. To their credit, the Penguins played well against us defensively and got ahead of us. We had a couple chances to score, but nothing too great. Time seems to be going so fast when you're trailing. We just couldn't tie the game. When the siren went off and we had lost, that was really difficult to swallow. It had been my decision to go to Detroit. Some people said that was karma for me as I decided not to re-sign with Pittsburgh. I had gotten so close again. That set up one of the toughest summers for me. My confidence was shaken and I was wondering how I was going to bounce back.

My parents had come in for the Stanley Cup Final again and I had lost again. After losing in Detroit, we went home and had a quiet dinner. It was Jana, me, my parents, my Slovakian agent Peter, and our dog. We had some dinner and drinks. It was quiet. After that, I got together with some guys from the team and ended up going to someone's house party. We all felt like it was a tough loss. I could tell the guys felt bad for me after I had lost the year before too.

I met with Babcock at the end of the season, and I could tell he was disappointed. The season before he was all excited to invite me to Detroit, but this had a different feeling. He said, "Well, Hoss, I don't know what's going to happen." He told me I needed to talk to Kenny. I didn't bother. I already knew I wasn't going to re-sign there. They didn't have the cap space for me.

I didn't understand it fully at the time, but being in Detroit was the best thing for me and my future. I was frustrated when we lost, especially having lost in the Stanley Cup Final two years in a row. But even though we didn't win the Cup, I learned so much that season. I'm able to put that into perspective now. It was so valuable in so many different ways being with that team and around those legends. I took all those things and applied them to the Blackhawks for the rest of my career. I wouldn't change anything about my experience in Detroit.

Six

There was this game Pavel Datsyuk and I used to play after nearly every Red Wings practice. One of us would have the puck and the other would have to try to take it off of them. You had to stay within the faceoff circle. We'd just go back and forth trying to take pucks off each other.

At first, I felt like a peewee player next to him. Pavel was so good. But I got better and better. Just playing that game helped me so much defensively. I had started improving as a two-way player in Atlanta. I was going more up and down the ice with Bob Hartley as coach and trying to set an example for the other guys. But I was still a 90-, 100-point player, so I was definitely still thinking more offense. But the change really started to occur when I went to Detroit on that one-year deal. There was Henrik Zetterberg there, too, and a lot of those guys played two-way hockey.

Before I arrived in Detroit, I had a lot of respect for Pavel, but it was different seeing him up close and in person, and especially playing that game in practice. He had so many tricks up his sleeve. He'd do one thing where he'd leave the puck next to him and protect it by having a strong stick. I would try to get it, but I just couldn't. With time, I started picking up those same tricks and using them in games. I'd put the puck beside me, and the opponent would come and I just protected it with my stick. Opponents don't expect that, where you'd have a really strong stick and have the puck moving beside you. They thought they could just grab the puck, but there was no way that was going to happen when I had my full strength protecting it. So Pavel taught me things like that. I got better at stealing pucks, protecting them, and backchecking. Even though we didn't win the Stanley Cup that season, there was so much I took from that one year and was able to benefit from and tap into when I went to the Blackhawks.

I even took that game with me to the Blackhawks. Teammates would see you doing it and they'd want to jump in. We'd have like seven guys in a circle playing. Everyone had a puck and you'd try to take it off each other. The player who loses the puck would leave the circle and there would be fewer and fewer players remaining. I think it was such a great game to learn how to better protect the puck or steal it. Those were great tools to put in your skill set. I'd have so much fun playing that game. Sometimes I couldn't wait for practice to end, just so we could play it.

As I mentioned, I did get better with time in that game. Eventually, I was taking pucks off Pavel. He didn't like that, though. He was really competitive. It's fun when you're getting better at something and you're really trying to work hard at it. It was nice to see the results.

Overall, I had a lot of respect for Pavel on and off the ice. When I arrived in Detroit, I had a seat right beside him in the dressing room. I think Mike Babcock did that because he knew he wanted to put us together on a line and wanted us communicating. Pavel was such a quiet guy. He was from Russia and I'm from Slovakia. I spoke a tiny bit of Russian, so I started using a few words with him. He liked that because not everybody speaks Russian. But then we got a little closer, hung out sometimes, and went to dinner. I just liked him because he was a quiet superstar. He never liked to be on center stage with the camera. He was more like, I'll show you what I can do on the ice, but leave me alone afterwards. He could score a hat trick or show some unbelievable skill, but he had no interest in doing the media. He just wanted to hide again. I respected that about him. He's still a superstar, but he could have been even bigger if he had a different personality. He liked to keep to himself and lead by example on the ice.

Pavel and I were on a line with Tomas Holmström for much of that season. We had so much fun together. Tomas would go in front of the net and make space for us. To this day, Homer was the best player I know at playing in front of the goalie. Pavel was doing all of his magic and then he'd give me the puck. I was shooting a lot of the time into a half-empty net because he took so much attention. He'd always pass the puck at the right moment. There haven't been many players I've played with who knew exactly when to pass it like he did. He was amazing. He made so many of those goals so easy for me to score.

Even though he was quiet in public, I did sometimes ask him about some of the things he did on the ice, and he'd be willing to explain it. I tried to do what he said and I found that I was improving. I've always loved to learn from the best. I do remember one year the under-20 World Championship was going on, and Russia was going to play Slovakia. He asked me if I wanted to bet some money on the game. I'm like, really? Russia had like seven first-rounders and Slovakia had one third-rounder. This is a fair bet to you? We were joking. His sense of humor was a little bit different, but I understood what he was trying to say. What he would say in broken English, you kind of got it a little bit later, and then you're like, that's actually funny. He had a different sense of humor, but he had such a good personality and was a great guy.

A lot of my appreciation for defense began with Pavel. I really got to enjoy stealing pucks. In games, I'd get my legs going and was reading the game. There'd be a pass from a defenseman to a forward and I'd be reading it. I'd want a good angle and have good speed. If I could get the right angle, I'd be able to close the gap quickly in front of me and I'd be able to catch them. It was a combination of a lot of different things. This is the NHL, too, so players aren't just giving you the puck. They can protect it well. It's not like playing peewee hockey and just lifting the stick. I picked up those tricks and learned how to steal pucks. As I did it more and more, I'm like, this is fun, and I really started enjoying it. Sometimes I enjoyed it more than going forward. I started skating harder to go backwards. My defensemen loved that too. For them, it made it easier to get the puck. I was happy to make it easier on them too.

After I left Detroit, it was always fun to play against Pavel. I remember one game specifically between Chicago and Detroit. Our lines would always play against each other. I knew when I had the puck that he was going to come for it like a shark out of nowhere. Whenever I touched the puck, it was like, where is No. 13, because the second I didn't see him, I knew it wasn't good. In this specific game, he took it away from me one time. I'm like, NO WAY, you're not going to get away with this. So I stopped, put my head down, and started

With two former teammates, Pavel Datsyuk and Evgeni Malkin, at the 2012 All-Star Game *(Getty Images)*

sprinting as fast as possible to take the puck away from him. He was my motivation in that shift. I was like, this puck is mine. And just as I learned from him, I lifted his stick by our blue line and took the puck from him and we started a new rush the other way. I came to the bench and felt like I had just scored a hat trick. What a feeling to steal the puck from the best.

Six

PAVEL WAS KIND enough to answer some of Scott's questions about our time together.

Q: What did you respect about Marián Hossa as a teammate?

Datsyuk: He always stayed positive on and off the ice. He was a true professional. He never showed that he was worried. He also was never afraid of the dirty work.

Q: Marián seemed to step into really good teams like Detroit, Pittsburgh, and Chicago and helped make them better. Is there a specific reason for that from your perspective?

Datsyuk: He was always a team player on any team. He respected the team's interest over his own.

Q: Marián talked about the game you and him would play trying to take the puck off each other. What do you remember about that?

Datsyuk: We enjoyed playing one-on-one very much. Sometimes others would join us too. It was a great time to forget about outside worries. We felt like we were kids again and made each other better.

Q: Marián said he learned a lot about playing two-way hockey from you. Do you feel like you passed anything on to him? Any elements of your game you eventually saw in him?

Datsyuk: I felt this for the first time after we started to play against each other on different teams.

Q: There was a Chicago-Detroit game where you took the puck off of him and he stole it back. Do you recall that?

Datsyuk: Marián read the game very well. He was very smart and fast with great hands. I am sure that happened.

Q: What was it like for you to see Marián have the team success he had with the Blackhawks after leaving Detroit?

Datsyuk: I was very concerned and worried for him the year we lost to Pittsburgh in the Final. I was very glad and happy when he finally won the Cup. He deserved to be a winner due to his professionalism.

Seven

I awoke the morning I won my first Stanley Cup wanting to treat the day as any other.

I had learned a number of valuable lessons from losing in the Stanley Cup Final the two previous years. One was not getting too far ahead of myself. Just the year before with the Red Wings, we had gone up 3–2, and I began to picture what the day of Game 6 could look like and envisioned myself lifting the Stanley Cup. It was like, wow, how close can you be, this could be the day that brings you the moment you dreamed of your whole life.

I didn't want to repeat that mistake. The Blackhawks' situation was eerily similar. We had won Game 5 in Chicago over the Philadelphia Flyers and were ahead 3–2 in the series. I realized I was in the same exact spot as I was with the Red

Wings, and I was conscious of trying to handle it differently this time.

My day didn't start perfectly. I didn't sleep great the night before. I turned off the TV and shut off the lights around my usual time, but my mind wouldn't follow the routine. It wasn't done racing about the possibilities of the next day. I eventually fell asleep. I woke up to my alarm the next day thinking, here we go, here's the day, OK, Hoss. My goal was to follow my game-day routine.

My mind just wasn't cooperating. You have voices in the back of your head telling you two different things. There's the one that is saying you should relax and be as normal as can be. The second voice is saying, OK, here we go again, what if you lose in the Stanley Cup Final three years in a row? Those were the kind of thoughts I was trying to block. I didn't want to think about what could, should, would happen. I wanted to hold those thoughts off.

I had my usual ham-and-cheese breakfast omelet. I felt good in the morning skate. The media, of course, asked me about possibly winning the Stanley Cup. After all, I was the only player to reach the Stanley Cup Final in three consecutive seasons with three different teams. It was a major storyline, but I didn't want to feed into it. I honestly don't remember what I told them because I was actively trying to be in the zone. I wasn't going to allow myself to worry about what could happen. Whatever was going to happen, I couldn't predict. It was going to happen anyways. I couldn't be concerned about it.

I went back to the hotel and hung out with the guys. Everyone was excited about the game. Everybody was careful to not say certain things, but you could sense the excitement. After our team lunch, I walked to the elevator with Jonathan Toews. Jonny turned to me and, "Hoss, just in case, be ready. Because if things go right tonight, you're going to be the first guy I give the Cup to." He caught me off guard. I didn't expect to hear that. I just said, OK. I didn't know what to say. I was usually careful not to say those types of things before big games. I didn't want to jinx anything. It was a short elevator ride in the Four Seasons hotel. I returned to my room thinking, this 22-year-old kid is so confident and was willing to say what he said. It ended up really helping me. It was amazing he told me that. It calmed me and allowed me to think about the game as any game and hope everything went right.

I took my pre-game nap, but that didn't go smoothly either. Instead of getting my 90 minutes of sleep, this nap lasted about 30 minutes. My mind wouldn't permit more than that. It was enough sleep, though. I was ready and able to focus.

I didn't see Jana before the game. She was just flying in for the game from Chicago. I didn't allow my parents to come. They had been there for the first Stanley Cup Final and I lost, and then the second Stanley Cup Final and I lost, so I told them, guys, sorry, you're not going to the third one. My dad understood. My mom was a little upset because she wanted to be there if I won, but she got it later. (My parents would be in attendance for the second Stanley Cup in 2013.)

I always sat in the second to the last row on the right side of the bus. Tazer was always in the last row. Kopy was in the row in front of me. Kane was in front of us to the left. Duncs was in back. Our team bus had a police escort to the stadium. There was a lot of traffic, but we flew right through it. When we got to the stadium, there's a lower deck for the bus and you could see people above it. You were just hoping no one would throw anything at you. They were booing us. You knew they weren't going to show us much hospitality. Philly fans are passionate.

I was in the zone for warmups. I went about it the same as I usually did, shooting from the same spots and so on. Obviously the fans in Philly were crazy, but we loved that atmosphere. You were prepared for anything. There were people booing and yelling things at you. There were signs. There was a poster where I was pictured sitting on the ice after losing in the Stanley Cup Final wearing a Pittsburgh jersey, then in a Detroit jersey, and they already had me in a Chicago jersey. You see those things while you're skating around. It's all part of the show. You either successfully block it or it's going to break you. Some of the signs were funny and you laugh at them.

After warmups, we had some time to ourselves. Ever since my early playing days in Slovakia, I'd say a short prayer before every game. I'm not a strictly religious person, but my wife and I were brought up that way and we'd go to church on Sundays, but let's be honest, not every Sunday. No one probably knew I was praying, but it was always part of my routine. It was a short prayer and always the same. I'd pray for a good result, good health, and maybe to score some goals and help the team to win.

Everyone else in the room was going about their routines too. Brent Seabrook had his unique one. He was talking routinely. At a certain point, he had to yell, and then he had to say something like at the seven-minute mark. Joel talked to us, but he kept it short. I always liked that about him. He didn't like long meetings, and neither did I. Everyone in the room understood what was at stake. Guys were telling me that this was the year and they were trying to get me going in a positive way. I was pretty positive too. I was ready for whatever was to come. I was ready for the challenge and ready to play big minutes. It wasn't easy because you did still have a weight on your shoulders. It never went away no matter how hard I tried to make it go away.

My body felt good. My knee was beat up from the game before. I had suffered a second-degree sprain of my MCL in Game 5. But I had been given a cortisone shot before warmups and that helped with the pain during the game. You'd feel it again after the game, but winning does help that too. I was also wearing a brace.

The game was back and forth. It was exciting for the fans. It was up and down. I played decent. I didn't score a goal, but Joel played me quite a bit, so I must have been doing something right. I was on a line with Kopy and Tazer. I was called for a goalie interference penalty in the second period. I was sitting in the penalty box, and those two minutes in a Final game were too long. It didn't feel like two minutes; it was way longer. There was a guy wearing a Flyers jersey and another guy next to him yelling, "Hossa, you're never going to win. You're cursed." I'm like, here we go again, another idiot. This guy was actually giving me fuel. I needed that. He woke me up. This was going to be my year and I was going to prove it to these people. Fortunately, we killed that penalty too.

We went down to the dressing room with the game tied after 60 minutes, and I was thinking this was as close as you can get. I knew Game 7 at home would have brought a lot of pressure. My other thought was, you could win it here and be done with it. I tried to relax, recharge for overtime, and bring my best again. I kept telling myself, don't "what if" again. I played the overtime with that attitude. You didn't want to make a mistake because you knew it could be costly and try to strike where you could. Kaner and the young guys probably thought about it differently than they would now. The response is different when you're a young, excited player. If you make a mistake, you don't think about it.

We didn't make that mistake, though. We won. Kaner made a great play, an unreal goal, almost from the side of the net in overtime. It's one of the craziest goals in Stanley Cup playoff history. When he scored, I was hanging on the boards. One leg was on the boards and the other was halfway on the ice. I'm like, did that puck really go through? It would have been a massive blow if the referees would have disallowed it. Half the bench was celebrating and half the bench was unsure. Instead of celebrating, I went to the referees. I said, "Guys, what's going on? Did it really cross the line?" They're like, "We're checking on it."

After they said it was a good goal, I felt the monkey come off my back immediately. All of a sudden, I started flying. The weight was gone. I felt so light. It was an amazing feeling when they said it was over. Kaner's goal meant so much to me, and I later told him that. It wasn't just a game-winner, but for myself, it freed me of being "cursed." That goal was golden for me.

We celebrated on the ice. There were a lot of Blackhawks fans there. The Philly fans were stunned. They couldn't believe it was a goal. The Flyers were still there standing on the bench wondering if we were still going to be playing some more. I was happy and jumping around, but I was also looking around and trying to take in the moment and enjoy it. When we went to get the Cup, I went around the penalty box to see if those guys who told me I was never going to win it were still there and show it to them. They weren't.

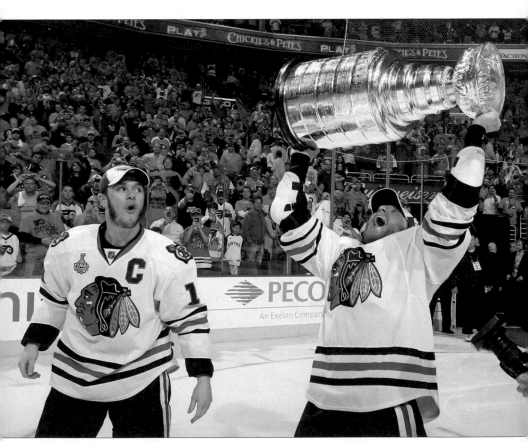

Finally! Hoisting the Stanley Cup in Philadelphia with Tazer *(Getty Images)*

Jonny picked up the Cup from NHL commissioner Gary Bettman, and I totally forgot what he had told me in the elevator earlier in the day. Everyone started yelling, "Hoss is here. Give it to Hoss." It was such a nice gesture by Jonny. It was most of the guys' first year in the Final, but they knew it was my third year in a row. It was a nice recognition from my teammates and Jonny to give it to me as the second guy. When he handed it to me, that first moment I touched the Cup and finally experienced the full weight of it, I didn't expect it to be as heavy as it was. I was like, wow. I thought it was going to be lighter. My second thought was, this is a dream come true. Philadelphia in 2010, this is the moment I've been waiting all my life for. After two unsuccessful finals, not years, but finals, this was a successful one. I was so happy that it had happened to me.

My favorite memories of winning the Stanley Cup came in the dressing room afterward. At first, everyone's in the room. It was a small visitors' room in Philly, but there were so many people packed in there. I didn't know a lot of them, but it didn't matter. Champagne was spraying left and right. After the media and others left, it was then just the trainers, coaches, and players, the group you're closest with, and the people you've just spent two months going to war with. That's the best feeling from all the Cups I've won. I have a great picture in my home with a stogie in my mouth and my wife sitting on my lap with the Cup. Kopy was sitting by us too. He and I played together in Detroit, and he told me before the Final that this would be the year we would win it together.

After I showered, I called my parents. They had watched the game in the middle of the night in Slovakia. I could hear the emotion in their voices and could imagine the tears in their eyes. I told them to pack their bags because they were coming to Chicago to celebrate with me. I wanted them to enjoy the atmosphere in Chicago too.

The flight home was crazy. Guys were drinking, enjoying the moment, and taking pictures with the Cup and Jonny's Conn Smythe Trophy. It was a fun flight back home. It felt

Jana and I with the Stanley Cup in Philadelphia

like a short flight. When we got to Chicago, there were lots of people waiting for us. There were two fire trucks that were spraying from opposite directions to create an arch of water. The plane drove through the gateway. It was a really cool way to recognize the Stanley Cup champions were back home. We then went to a restaurant near O'Hare Airport to celebrate.

We were so tired after that. It had been two long months of the playoffs and three very long seasons for me. We had been drinking some. Some of the young guys went out late until the morning. Jana and I were so tired after an hour. We took the car and went home. I needed my rest, too, because I had told Jana that because this was my third Final in a row,

With Tomáš Kopecký and his wife, Maria

I was going to make a statement if we won: I was going to celebrate hard for five days. She was like, you can do it. That was the first night. By the third night, I was getting tired, but I said, "I told you I would do it five nights. I promised that." On my last night, guys were going out and I was so tired that I didn't want to go out at all. But I promised myself, you have to enjoy five nights. That night, I almost fell asleep standing in one spot. It wasn't even from drinking. I was so tired. I'm like, "Hoss, you better go home." But I did my five nights, as I promised my wife, and, most importantly, myself.

That first night I went home early. It was like 2 a.m. You want to party, but you just can't. You're exhausted and want to go to bed. Some of the younger guys felt differently. Maybe when I was 20, 21, I would have been thinking the same thing. When you look at it, I was in the Final and on the road for three straight seasons. I was physically and mentally tired. I felt like I needed a good night of sleep to then party five nights straight.

WHAT I LEARNED from losing those first two finals and finally winning was to never give up. Never give up on your dreams. The first time didn't work out. I was really close the second time, but it didn't work out again. When that third time came, I was more prepared, but I was also hungrier and determined to prove I could do it. There may have been people who thought I was cursed and thought of me as a loser, but I knew I was a winner and I could do it. There are definitely voices in your head that want to make you question yourself, but I didn't let them take over me. I knew I trained hard. I knew we had a great team. It's not always going to work out and you may take some losses and some bumps along the way, but you have to work through that and persevere. Good things will happen eventually, even when you're least expecting it. I always kept looking forward and believing. During the playoffs someone had given me a small prayer card that had a picture of Jesus on one side and text on the other. I put it in my wallet and looked at it every time things weren't going as I would have liked in the playoffs.

I awoke the morning after I won my first Stanley Cup knowing the day would be unlike any other. I woke up really early that next day. I was getting bombed with messages from people back home in Slovakia. I tried to sleep, but I couldn't. I thought I was going to sleep until 10 a.m., but I was up at 6 a.m. and I was fresh. I'm like, what the hell? My wife was still sleeping. I went into the other room, made some coffee, and sat on the couch. I couldn't believe it had really happened. It was the best feeling ever. You just start enjoying the moment actually. Maybe some people who win it right away don't feel that way. But for me, after three times, it was too long. You appreciate it more. I felt so strong that morning. You're supposed to be tired, but I wasn't. I felt like I had the energy to play another game because I just won. I felt unbelievable that morning. It was almost like I could have started drinking at 6:30 a.m. But I didn't. That came later.

Eight

Even at a young age, there was always something special about the Chicago Blackhawks for me. And as I got older, those connections seemed to only grow. It felt like fate that I ended up there.

Knowing I wasn't likely returning to Detroit, my agent, Ritch, helped compile a research book on all the possible teams I could sign with during the summer of 2009. He did an excellent job with that, and I started studying it. We wanted to have a good idea of where I could possibly sign before July 1. We knew quickly there weren't that many teams that fit my criteria, maybe a handful. When I saw Chicago was one of the possibilities, I got excited. I did always have those strange connections to the franchise. I had a Steve Larmer jersey when I was a kid. I had played in juniors for the Portland Winterhawks, which had the same logo as the Blackhawks.

Plus, they were an Original Six team and possessed a lot of talent. There was potential there. If they wanted me and were willing to give me a long-term deal, I thought they could be a fit. Honestly, once I started thinking about Chicago as my destination, I was hoping it would be them.

The Tampa Bay Lightning were the other team pushing for me. They came in with a strong offer too. The length and salary—12 years, $63.3 million—were the same as the Blackhawks' offer. If I'm being truly honest, the weather and the taxes are better in Florida. But my gut told me Chicago was going to be a better fit. I did consider how great it would have been to raise my family in a warmer location. But I was worried about the Lightning's ownership at the time, and I had already experienced something like that in Atlanta. There were a number of factors playing in the Blackhawks' favor.

My No. 1 objective signing that offseason above anything else was winning a Stanley Cup. To do that, I knew I needed to play for a good team. Secondly, I wanted a long-term contract and a no-movement clause, to give my family stability and security. The Blackhawks provided those things, and I was happy to sign with them because I knew they had the potential to be a really good team for a long time. They weren't experienced yet, but they had talent. They were a team on the rise. They had great young players and a great coaching staff with Joel Quenneville as their head coach. There was also a lot of interest in hockey in Chicago again. It had been pretty dead for a while there. I remember thinking in the past, what's wrong with this city? There was no one coming to games. They had been bad and no one seemed to really want to play there. That, of course, had changed.

The length of the contract was something Ritch and I discussed before free agency. I was entering my 30s and getting older, but I looked at someone like Chris Chelios, and he was still playing as he got up there in age. I also weighed the facts that I liked to work out, was in great shape, and hadn't had any major injuries in my career. It wasn't like I partied or didn't take care of myself. I mostly stayed home and tried to be a true professional. For all those reasons, I told Ritch I

My family and I along Lake Michigan in Chicago

wanted to seek a longer contract. I thought I could play into my 40s as long as nothing serious happened to me. I don't remember worrying then whether I'd be able to play out my entire 12-year contract. It really wasn't a thought.

Dale Tallon was the Blackhawks general manager at the time. I never thought he got enough credit for building what that team became with how he drafted, developed players, and signed free agents. In my case, he had the confidence to sign me to such a long-term deal. He believed I could help the Blackhawks for a long time. I always respected and liked Dale. I still keep in touch with him to this day. Stan Bowman took over for him and kept the team strong for a long time. It was basically a new era in Chicago. We had created a dynasty. Meeting Stan's dad, Scotty Bowman, in Chicago for the first time was special too. He's a legend and a huge persona in the hockey world, and obviously has the most wins in NHL history. It was cool to talk to him about hockey and discuss all his Stanley Cup rings.

AS EXCITED AS I was to sign with the Blackhawks, I did have some potentially bad news for them at the start. I found out I needed surgery on my right arm after playing in the Stanley Cup Final the season before with Detroit. I basically couldn't shoot or hold any weight with my right arm. It was so weak. I knew if I wanted to perform at a high level going forward,

I needed to get it fixed. I also realized I had to be honest and upfront with the Blackhawks about it. Ritch thought the same. We knew it would look bad if I signed and then told them I needed surgery. So, the Blackhawks knew going in I might require surgery that offseason.

The Blackhawks had also added Tomáš Kopecký that offseason. I was excited to have another Slovak on the team. Kopy and I flew to Chicago that July for the Blackhawks convention. While I was there, we had a big meeting about my arm. It felt like the whole organization was in this meeting about whether I should have surgery. I couldn't believe it. John McDonough, Jay Blunk, Scotty Bowman, Stan Bowman, the trainers, coaches, everyone was there. They started talking about what we could do. The meeting was about an hour. I almost started sweating because I was answering so many questions. They didn't want to look bad in front of the public, because they had just signed this long-term deal with a high-profile player and here I was about to possibly announce right away I was having surgery.

I told them I needed the surgery, and it would be better for me in the long run. I said I'd be ready for the middle of the season and be stronger as the playoffs approached. Team president John McDonough asked me if I could get through the whole season and then have the surgery. I was worried about that. There was no guarantee that it wouldn't deteriorate, and then I'd risk being home for the playoffs. Someone mentioned there was a clinic in Minnesota that was doing a procedure with an electrical current that might be able to help me. It was Accelerated Recovery Performance (ARP). They recommended going to Minnesota and seeing if it could be done in two weeks. I thought it was the least I could do considering the contract they were giving me. So, Blackhawks conditioning coach Paul Goodman and I traveled to Minnesota.

As I expected, if you're dealing with something as serious as I was dealing with, there wasn't some magical fix to it. Still, I tried the electrical current therapy. I did it for the full week and flew back to Chicago. I told them it was the same. I grabbed something and my arm wasn't strong enough to hold it.

We ended up doing the surgery in Chicago. Dr. Mike Terry did an excellent job. Ultimately, I think that really helped me with my strength. I was also watching every game at home really closely while I was rehabbing and studying how the team was playing. I wanted to get back as quickly as possible. The guys were winning. I just wanted to blend in and help us keep winning. My conditioning was really good too.

Finally the day came when I started skating with my new team for the first time. I was skating up and down the ice as fast as anyone. I wasn't getting tired either. Q told me that was how he wanted me to play because the guys were seeing me put in the effort. That time training with Pauly when I was injured definitely helped me that season play my game at a high level.

When I initially arrived in Chicago, I knew Joel Quenneville as a good D-man with 800-plus career NHL games and as a successful NHL coach. He had already won so many games. I also already knew he was a players' coach, and I have always liked that style of coach because they usually know how a player feels. I don't have anything against other types of coaches, but a players' coach usually can sense when things aren't going right, whether you need a day off after a lot of travel, and just those sort of things. I was right about Joel. He did seem to always know exactly how the players felt. For a lot of reasons, he was my favorite coach to ever play for in the NHL. I wasn't alone. A lot of guys loved to play for him. He understood us. He'd also do the small things for us, like give us days off or push for a Las Vegas trip for the team every season.

I remember meeting Joel for the first time after I signed with the Blackhawks. We met at the reception during the Blackhawks convention that summer. I went up to the third floor where we had a special check-in for the team and Joel was there, waiting in line. I said, "Hey, Joel, nice to meet you." He had a big smile under his thick mustache. He said, "Hoss, welcome, you're gonna love it here. And we're gonna have a lot of fun together." I thought to myself, this is a guy I want to play for. And you know what? He was right. We did have a lot of fun.

I never got into any arguments with Joel. There was one time late in my career where I didn't think he was playing me enough and I told him that in a friendly way. There was always respect in the way we talked. His door was always open. I didn't go in there much, but when we talked, it was honest. We had played in Boston during the Father-Son road trip and Joel had played me just 12 minutes. It was the least amount of ice time I had ever received from him. I wasn't happy at all. We had won the game 1–0 and I scored the lone goal, but I still wasn't happy. I told him I felt like I was playing well and felt good and he wasn't using me enough. I was starting to worry that if I wasn't playing the minutes I was used to, my legs wouldn't be the same and I wouldn't be able to help our team as I was accustomed to when I played a lot. He just told me his side of the story and then we shook hands. That's how it's supposed to be. It really wasn't anything big, but we had a good talk. I understand the coach can't play everyone as much as they want. I just tried to treat people with respect and I think I got the same thing in return.

During that convention was also the first time I obviously met with my new teammates. We got together in one of the hotel rooms. I remember it being so crowded. There were guys joking and jumping on the bed. They opened one of the windows and started throwing stuff out of it. I stood back, watched, and started laughing. It was like a junior team. I had just come from Detroit where I was drinking wine with Nick Lidström and Chris Chelios. There, it had been really calm, and everyone had their own kids. And then I came to a team like Chicago, and they were like kids themselves. They were jumping on the bed, making a mess, doing pranks. I thought to myself, this is fun, this is going to be great. That's how it was on the ice too.

We had a lot of fun in a lot of different places. Those Vegas trips were definitely part of that fun. There wasn't a team in Vegas then, so every other team in the league didn't understand why we were taking those trips. It was really rare, but we were given some perks by the team's owner, Rocky Wirtz, and the front office. I'm not sure how the trips started, but Joel definitely had something to do with it. The good thing was we were winning most of the time around those Vegas trips. Everyone would always look forward to it. That was like a getaway in the middle of the season. It was nice to break up the season and not just do the same thing for 82 games. You did want to make sure before and after the trip you were playing well, because you knew ownership was trying to figure out whether this was a good idea or not. It obviously cost ownership some money, but they knew the team was going to enjoy it and it would bring us closer together. We'd have the rookie party during the trip. Everybody had dinner together. We'd hang out by the pool and have some long sessions in the casino. I'd go to some shows with the trainers. Everybody was relaxed those two nights.

There was one year before the trip to Vegas that we got killed in Edmonton. The score was like 7-2. Not good at all. It was a quiet flight to Vegas. The bus arrived at the Bellagio and Joel got up and politely told everybody to get off the bus except for the players. When they had, Joel stood up in the aisle and started yelling: "Tonight's performance was horse-shit and an embarrassment! You guys should be ashamed of yourselves and you better be ready for the next game. But now, now we are in Vegas, and I want you to enjoy it. So go and have fun these three days." That was Joel. Unreal, right?

Playing Nintendo and *Mario Kart* was a big thing with our team when he hit the road for the playoffs. I began watching the other guys play and then decided to give it a try. It was fun to bump into other guys on the big screen. I wasn't the best. I was probably somewhere in the middle. After I stopped playing, I'd just watch it and laugh. The other guys were so into it. I was at the age where I had stopped playing video games pretty much.

Patrick Sharp and Adam Burish liked to play other types of games too. They were big into pranks. I recall them trying to play one on me once. We were playing somewhere and flew into New Jersey late. We are on the bus on the way to the hotel. Burish was among the first to get off the bus and got my hotel key. While that was happening, Sharpie was stalling me and talking to me at the back of the bus. That gave him a good alibi too. Smart, right? I picked up my key, went to my room, and everything was a mess. I was pretty sure who did it, but I played it cool. I slowly gathered some information and found out it was them.

Later on, we were playing in Dallas, and I got Sharp and Burish's room key. I got in touch with Kaner, who was going to dinner with the two of them. The plan was for Kaner to call or text me when they were returning. While they were gone, I undid their beds, filled up a bucket of water, dumped it on their mattresses, and remade them as if they had never been touched. When they came back, Kaner told me Burish sat on his bed and was like, "Holy fuck, this is wet." He started blaming Sharp. Those guys didn't trust each other with the pranks. They found out it was me later on, but I didn't own up to it. I'm like, what are you talking about? It was priceless, though. I'm not sure how they slept on those mattresses. All I know is I slept well that night.

I HAVE SO many great memories from my time in Chicago. I obviously already devoted a whole chapter to winning my first Stanley Cup. I also have another chapter on playing with

Jonathan Toews and Patrick Kane. They're both such special players. I also wrote a chapter on the dramatic hit by Raffi Torres on me and the skin condition that ended my career.

So, what else to discuss?

For me, our dramatic opening-round series with the Predators in 2010 was so memorable. My dream could have ended there again. When I took that boarding penalty late in Game 5 of the conference quarterfinals, I honestly wasn't sure if it was the right call. Maybe it was boarding? I didn't want to hurt the guy. We were down late, we had pulled the goalie, dumped the puck into the corner, and I was just chasing the guy. I was trying to win the battle. It's not like I crushed him in the head and he fell down, so it's kind of just one of those moments.

As I sat in the penalty box, all I could do was hope they didn't score another goal. And then somehow magically Kaner scored shorthanded. The United Center went crazy. But the worst part was there was still a lot of time left in my penalty even as we went to overtime. In the dressing room, I was just praying that we'd kill the penalty. When overtime started, the ice was clean and they were on the power play. They had some good players, especially Shea Weber with his big shot, on their power play unit. I wasn't moving in the penalty box. I was still just praying. Every time we threw the puck to their zone, I took a deep breath. I can laugh about it today, but it would have been a different story if Nashville had scored.

Just before my penalty ended, we were spending time in their zone. I jumped out of the box and joined them. Dave Bolland passed the puck to Brent Sopel at the top of the zone, and Sopel shot it on net. I entered the zone and went straight to the net. I saw we had the coverage. I was trying to get to the net and make something happen. The puck bounced right in front of me, and I was in a perfect position. My eyes were so big. I saw the half-empty net and had this great opportunity to shovel the puck into it. That's what I did.

When I saw the puck go in and red light go off, I just reacted. I'm not even sure why I celebrated like I did, because I never get on two knees like it. It just came naturally. It was such a relief to go from sweating in the penalty box to scoring a big goal. We went up 3–2 in that series and won it in six games. I've found the first round is sometimes the hardest one because both teams are flying around, have energy, and no one is too beat up yet. That was one of the toughest rounds that season. After that game, I think we knew we could do something special. We didn't know how far we'd go, but we started having more confidence and began rolling.

Rolling all the way to the Stanley Cup that season was just the start of an amazing time for me. Jana and I were married later that summer in Slovakia. We did have a bit of an

all our friends and family there. Jana looked stunning in the dress we nearly left in Chicago. As the guests were leaving at about 4 a.m., there was a huge thunderstorm that came through. That felt like a fitting end to what was a perfect day.

THREE YEARS LATER, I was back in the Stanley Cup Final. In our 2013 Stanley Cup run, it wasn't so much the first round but the second round that gave us trouble. We were down 3–1 to my former team, the Red Wings. We had rolled through the regular season and won the Presidents' Trophy. Expectations were high again, but you never know in the playoffs.

With us facing elimination, we had an off day between games and held a team meeting. We knew they thought they had us. We started talking about not worrying about where we were in the series. Other teams were already at home. We were in the conference semifinals. We were down to one more loss but we still had a chance, and that was more than those other teams. We tried to look at the positives, take it day by day, see what happens, and bring everything we could to the next game. We tried to think of it as the pressure being on them to close the series.

Joel put some great lines together and we started producing. We won Game 5. Michael Frolík scored a big penalty shot in Game 6 to help us even the series. We went home for Game 7. We thought we had the game-winning goal by Niklas

Hjalmarsson, but it was disallowed and went to overtime. Seabs finally scored the big goal to win it. We were definitely facing adversity and elimination and the whole team put everything together. It was unreal to beat them coming back from 3–1 down in the series.

One of the worst injuries of my career came during the Stanley Cup Final later during that playoff run. It was Game 2 against the Boston Bruins, and I was cross-checked by my good friend Zdeno Chára. The injury was somewhat of a fluke. He just gave me a little shot in the back, but he hit me in a weird way. I started feeling something was wrong immediately. I went to sit on the bench and I could feel something shooting down my leg. I knew something wasn't right. I wasn't mad at Z because obviously that's his style. He doesn't care if you're his neighbor in Slovakia or some other guy; later on in the book, he'll explain that himself. That's just his style. It wasn't even a hard cross-check. It was just weird. It was unexpected. I was just skating by and he cross-checked me. I wasn't in pain, but I felt something moving within my body. It felt like my body had been shifted into a different position. It definitely started causing a problem.

After the game, I told our trainer Jeff Thomas about it. I had never had a problem with my back. I was like, what the hell? I went to bed that night in Chicago after we won. We were supposed to fly to Boston the next day. In the morning, I called JT and told him I couldn't sit down. I didn't know how I was even going to drive to the airport. He asked if he should pick me up. I said, please, because I had something shooting down my leg and I would have to drive sideways to get into a comfortable position. I couldn't believe it. I thought, why now? I'm in the Final. I got into his car on the passenger side and I was like sitting all the way to the side. He's like, is it that bad? I'm like, yeah. He could see my face and me shifting around.

At the airport, we saw Dr. Mike Terry and told him what was happening. They decided to set up a shot for me because the pain was starting to increase rapidly. So we got to Boston and the three of us saw a specialist that could give me a cortisone shot in the back. Nobody knew about it. I was in real pain. Usually, you're supposed to take a break for a period after the shot, at least a few days or a week. You're not supposed to do anything. But we had a game the next day. I told them I didn't feel right at all.

That night, I couldn't sleep on my bed. I pulled the sheets off the mattress and slept on the floor. It was getting worse. I tried to put my socks on and I couldn't. I had Game 3 in front of me and I could barely move. The team had the morning skate, and I didn't even bother going. Before the game, they gave me an epidural steroid injection, so I wouldn't feel the pain. It's the playoffs, so these type of shots could keep you from feeling certain things and you could play the game.

And then after the game, you would start feeling worse. The important thing was you were able to play the game, and because you were that far in the playoffs, you were willing to do that. So I had the cortisone shot the day before and then the second shot to reduce the pain.

I thought all that was going to work, but still something wasn't right. I couldn't bend over to tie my skates. I had a trainer tie my skates. I thought he had tied them too tight because after I got the second shot I couldn't feel my leg. It was numb. I went to the trainers' room right before warmups, and I told them, "This is not right. I don't feel my leg. It might be tingling." I did want to play. We were so close again to another Stanley Cup. The first Stanley Cup run I had a problem with my knee, my MCL, and put a brace on. With some things, you're like, OK, fuck it. But this was different.

I tried it out, though. I was excited like everyone else for warmups. I got behind Kaner to jump on the ice. It was a superstition of mine. I jumped on the ice and nearly fell down. I felt like I was on one leg out there. I could feel my left leg, but it was like my right leg wasn't mine. I had never felt that way in my life. I was skating around and it felt like I was skating on one leg. I just stood there. I told the guys what I was feeling, because obviously the cameras and media were watching. They said just to stand there during the warmups and they'd talk to the coaches about a decision. I told them, seriously, I would be so useless for this game because I couldn't even skate. They eventually decided to pull me from the game. I went to my hotel room and watched the game while I sat on my floor. I felt terrible because I wanted to do something to help, but I couldn't do anything. The shot didn't work. My whole leg was numb. How are you supposed to play on one leg?

I wasn't worried about the long-term effects of the shots. I knew a lot of players took these shots to ease the pain. You don't take them during the regular season because you don't want all that stuff in your body all the time. But when you're in the playoffs and close to a Stanley Cup, you're willing to do anything for the team to win. You don't know when you'll get another chance. That's hockey. That's professional sports. That's part of it.

The next game, my leg was pretty much the same, maybe 10 percent better. There was still a weird feeling. I was willing to try again, because we had lost Game 3 and I really wanted to help the team. Joel said to me, "Look, I need you to be in the lineup. I want the other team to see your name in there." I told him it felt a little bit better, but it was going to be 50 percent less of Marián Hossa out there. He's like, "Well, 50 percent less is better than none." I said, that's fair, but don't expect me to do many things because I am limited right now and I mean it. I don't want to be, but I am. Whatever happened to the disc in my back, it was shooting a pain through my leg. Even when I was eating with the team, I couldn't sit in my chair right.

I did feel better before Game 4. I could step on my leg and feel it, but I still wasn't myself. I didn't feel like I wanted to, not even close. I was just bracing myself for the game. I didn't want to make any mistakes and just keep it simple. I told the guys, I'm just going to pass the puck and probably keep my shifts as short as possible. That's basically how I played. I felt small and hopeless, but we won Game 4 in overtime.

Come Game 5, I felt better and we won that one too. In Game 6, I was feeling even better. I still wasn't myself, but I felt so much better than before. As that game went on, I was starting to get some movement again. It started feeling more comfortable. It was such a relief, not just physically but also mentally, because I had felt like I was stuck in someone else's body. I had read what Tony Amonte had said on TV during the series, about having to sacrifice for the team and how I wasn't because I was out with an injury. The trainers were upset with him because he was a former Blackhawks player. It bugged me, too, because I wanted to play, but I couldn't. I said hopefully we win and I can say something to him. The poor guy didn't have a clue what was going on, so I just let it go. Plus, I had better things to do after we won—celebrate.

I was still feeling something in my back after the series. It was probably another week and a half before I started feeling better. I got another shot in Chicago after we won the Stanley Cup and got another one in Slovakia, so I did have to get a few different shots over time because it didn't feel perfect yet. The pains weren't as sharp. It certainly wasn't as bad as before, where I felt like I had glass in my body and I was hitting a nerve every time I moved. It got slowly better. I was pretty worried because I had never felt anything like that. You hear about those injuries and sometimes people having to have surgery. I would have had the surgery if needed, but that was going to be my last option. Thank God I didn't need a surgery. I did need those additional cortisone shots, though.

THAT 2013 SERIES, of course, will always be remembered for the two goals we scored in 17 seconds in Game 6. What I remember is we were down by a goal in what had been a real tough game, and the clock was ticking on us. It looked like there might have to be a Game 7. I was sitting on the bench for what happened next.

Joel pulled the goalie to get us six players out there. Bryan Bickell, who is a big body and had a great playoffs, was out there. Tazer, Kaner, and, I think, Michal Handzuš, another big body, were on the ice as well. Somehow Bickell scored and the game was tied. The fourth line jumped on the ice for the next shift. We were in a good mood on the bench. While we were enjoying that feeling, BOOM, we scored again. This time it was Dave Bolland. We had scored twice in 17 seconds, and it's like, what the hell just happened? We couldn't believe it. We hadn't even sat down from celebrating the first goal. The building just went quiet. You could hear a pin drop. And for us, we were jumping around like little kids on the bench. We couldn't believe we had scored two goals like that in what had been such a tight game.

I was so happy for guys like Zus, Michal Rozsíval, and Jamal Mayers who were able to win the Stanley Cup that season. I finally got my first one in 2010, but those guys had never experienced it before, and you didn't know how much longer they'd be around in the league. As much as others wanted to win the Cup for me when I hadn't before, I wanted to win it for them too. When we acquired Zus at the trade deadline, GM Stan Bowman had asked me about him. I had played with him on the national team. I told Stan he was a great character guy and would fit well in the dressing room. He played great for us and helped us win the Cup that season.

One of my favorite memories from the Cup celebration in Boston was grabbing a champagne bottle, taking it to the coaches' office, and spraying it all over Q. There's this great picture of me, Q, and Andrew Shaw all wet from the champagne. I remember Q saying what a great feeling it was to win and this was why you played hockey, or something like that.

It was fun to see the coaches having fun and really enjoying themselves too.

I was still sweating long after that game ended. I took a shower and was still sweating. Everyone was starting to get on the bus to leave. I jumped in the cold tub to cool down and it hit me exactly what we had done. I got out and began dressing. I started walking out of the TD Garden to the bus and

I was behind the camera for a change when we visited the White House after winning the Stanley Cup in 2013. I'm taking a picture of the Blackhawks trainers—these guys deserve so much credit! *(Getty Images)*

my brother and Marián Gáborík called me on FaceTime. That was cool to be holding the Stanley Cup, walking to the bus, and talking to my friends and family who were back home still celebrating in Slovakia. I showed them the Stanley Cup and told them I'd be bringing it back to Trenčín.

TWO YEARS LATER, I was lucky enough to win the Stanley Cup for a third time. What was so great about us winning the Cup in 2015 was we had very little drama in the series-clinching win against Tampa. We built a little cushion in Game 6 and were really able to enjoy everything late in that game. In Philly and Boston, it came right down to the wire. In this one, we were able to celebrate a little bit before the game ended. It was also great that we clinched the Cup at home for the first time. We didn't have to board a plane afterward. I'll get more into it later in the book, but it was great having Jana and my brother there for that Cup and celebrating it with him for the next few days.

Being able to celebrate before our home fans was amazing that third time. Blackhawks fans were great throughout my career. They sold out the United Center every game, and you could always feel a buzz in the air. When I was hurt and wasn't playing, I'd be up in the press box and got to take it all in from a different perspective. You'd look around and feel this energy coming from the crowd. From my first game to my last, that was always there. It was such an energetic crowd whether you scored a goal and "Chelsea Dagger" began playing or during the legendary singing of the national anthem. During the playoffs, it was at another level. It'd be hard to hear anything other than the crowd. You didn't see or hear that anywhere else other than in Chicago. It was definitely unique. There were those times that the crowd would chant, "Hossa! Hossa! Hossa!" That always made me feel good. One of my most memorable fan interactions came following that 2015 Stanley Cup victory. We had been at one of the local bars, and there was this woman wearing a "Bitches Love Hossa" T-shirt. Someone pointed it out to me, and I took a picture with her. It was pretty hilarious.

There were seven of us that won all three Stanley Cups together. Back home in my garage, I have a framed photo with six of us together after winning the Stanley Cup that final time. In the picture, there's Tazer, Kaner, Duncs, Seabs, Sharpie, and myself. I'm not sure where Hammer was for the photo. I devoted an upcoming chapter to Kaner and Tazer, but I wanted to discuss those other guys too. They were special players as well.

Duncan Keith, "The Wolf," was the first guy to invite Kopy and me to dinner when I arrived in Chicago in 2009. I thought, wow, that's really nice. We went to dinner and talked about the team, the city, the coaching staff, management, and everything else. He had a lot of positive things to say, and we had a great time. As a player, he was really professional and willing to do anything to win and be prepared. He loved to train. He always came to training camp in the best shape. He was a great teammate and person, but his personality could also change on a dime. He could be happy one moment and then go crazy the next, but I loved being his teammate and have a lot of great memories. I don't think I've ever seen someone wear more skates in my life than him. But he won the Norris Trophy twice, so something must have worked.

Brent Seabrook was the fire in the room. He'd be one of the first guys there and he'd be talking and talking and talking. He was firing up the room and making jokes. He was really outspoken. When things weren't going right, we needed someone like him. He'd make our dressing room more relaxed and allow us to play our game. He's such a great person and I enjoyed having him around. He scored some big goals, especially as a defenseman. When the big time came, he showed up and scored some key goals for us in the playoffs. That's something you never forget.

Patrick Sharp was in Chicago for a really long time. He was a real steady star. He had great shooting ability. I spent some time on the same line with him and I respected him as a person and player. He accomplished so much and proved himself as a star in the league. He's been great on TV after retiring from hockey. He knows what he's talking about. He always knew the staff and players. He did always like to be right all the time. Sharpie was a great teammate.

Niklas Hjalmarsson was a calm Swedish guy. He was our defensive, stay-at-home defenseman. He was a super nice guy and would do anything for the team. We had a lot of success because of him too. He was a great guy in the locker room. He was obviously a warrior on the ice. I never saw him complain about anything. He showed so much character and that was unbelievable.

We were successful in Chicago not just because of the players. The whole training and equipment staff were great in Chicago too. They were important as well. Mike Gapski, one of the oldest trainers in the NHL, played a huge role in the dressing room. I mentioned before how Jeff Thomas went above and beyond his job for me. All of our equipment staff, including Troy Parchman, was there for me throughout those years. Jim Heintzelman took care of my sticks and did an excellent job.

I was obviously devasted to hear when Clint Reif, another one of our trainers, died. We heard what happened after playing the Columbus Blue Jackets. It was really sad. You think everything is fine, but you just really never know with a person. It's hard to accept what happened. I remember coming to the dressing room and everyone was so quiet. I couldn't believe when I heard. I felt so bad for his family. Clint had always been there for me with my sticks and equipment. He was close to us. Those trainers are so important to us as players. We need them and we try to make sure they're taken care of too. Clint was always there for me. He'd prepare my sticks for every game. I knew if something was wrong, I could call him and have it fixed fast.

Paul Goodman helped me throughout my time in Chicago too. As I got older, I did start feeling different. Maybe around when I was 30, I could tell my recovery took longer. I would need to do more to recover. I started using Pauly's workout program in the summer instead of mine around when I was 35. I talked to Pauly quite a bit during the summer about his program and we were in touch way more often than my previous years with the Blackhawks. My routine was doing legs and core one day and then upper body and core the next day. It was a nice, basic program. In the evening, I'd go run or play tennis, soccer, or inline hockey. I did that whole routine for much of my career. When I went to Pauly's program, it was totally different with new exercises and a different program that was on a computer. What I did to help me adjust was I hired my buddy Brando Kvetan to be my training coach. I told him I'd pay him to train me, but he had to prepare with the program that Pauly sent. He'd study the program and be ready for when I trained. That worked out well for me. That new program brought some excitement to me, too, instead of just doing what I had done by myself. I trusted Pauly because he's a great strength coach.

Being with the Blackhawks, I had the privilege to get to know Stan Mikita a bit. There are only three players from Slovakia who have scored 500 NHL goals, and all three played for the Blackhawks. There was Peter Bondra, Stan Mikita, and me. That's pretty cool. Stan was born in Slovakia and went to Canada when he was eight years old. I remember meeting Stan for the first time in 2009. He was an ambassador for the Blackhawks and obviously a huge legend. It was right around when I signed. It was a special moment meeting him. I'd see him many times over the years. We'd always share a few words in Slovak. He was really polite and down to earth.

One time I was asked if I'd go with Stan to visit a young boy name Ross MacNeill. Stan and I were in the car together for like an hour. We talked about everything, including Slovakia. He told me stories from the old days. He was just the same guy all the time. He was just so normal. I'll never forget that trip. It was sad. Ross was diagnosed with an aggressive brain tumor, but he was so happy to see us. You could see the spark in his eyes. Stan and I talked to his parents for a while. I couldn't imagine what they were going through. It put life in a different perspective. It made me realize you needed to be happy with what you have and your health. Obviously later on, I found out Stan had dementia. I saw his wife, Jill, at one of the Christmas parties and she said he wasn't doing well. I was emailing with his daughter later on about coming to see him, but she said he probably wouldn't remember me. I decided it was probably best to remember him as I did before.

I'M SO HAPPY for everything that happened in Chicago. The only thing I might have also liked in my career was an individual trophy. I had been close with the Calder Trophy, but I didn't play the full season with Ottawa as a rookie. The Selke would have been nice too. I thought there was one season with the Blackhawks I might have a chance with that because of my plus-minus, backchecking, and penalty-killing ability, but I didn't get many votes because I didn't play center. There was one summer where I started thinking about working on my faceoffs to enable me to play some center too. Maybe voters would consider me then. But that didn't happen because I played on a line with Jonny and he always won the faceoffs. The Selke was an award that went to centers. I'm not sure why that is in the National Hockey League. They should call it a center's trophy or something, because you have great defensive wingers and they're not even considered. It definitely sucks for wingers.

Two of the most special moments for me in Chicago were being honored for playing 1,000 NHL games and for scoring 500 career goals. The first one, the 1,000 games, I remember thinking how cool it was to be on the red carpet and having all those people cheering for you. I received a commemorative silver stick during that ceremony. The 500 goals ceremony was even more special. It was a larger ceremony and a greater accomplishment. I was presented a golden stick during that.

On the ice at the United Center to celebrate my 500 career goals

I also had nearly my entire family present in Chicago for the 500-goal ceremony. Unfortunately, my brother couldn't make it because he was still playing. But my wife, children, and parents were all there. I have a big picture from that night in my office. I have so many amazing photos from that evening. It's one thing to be able to have your family there to watch you play, but to have them on the red carpet on the ice with me for that was so special. It's something I'll never forget.

Although I was the one being honored, it was Zoja, my youngest daughter, who stole the show during the ceremony when she honked my nose. The whole building was laughing. Funny story about that was John McDonough had told me he was afraid he wouldn't be able to say my name correctly when he first signed me because my name was somewhat close to "Sosa," and he had worked for so long with the Chicago Cubs and their star player Sammy Sosa. So during my 500-goal ceremony, it was John who was talking on the microphone when Zoja honked my nose. John didn't know that happened behind him and all of a sudden he began to hear everyone laughing. His first thought was he had messed up and accidentally called me Sosa instead of Hossa.

I was really honored to be recognized for both those accomplishments. It's hard to describe what it means to reach those milestones. You don't exactly set out to achieve them. Growing up, I always wanted to play in the National Hockey

League. And then, that starts with the goal of getting drafted. Once you're drafted and in training camp, you want to make the team and establish a position for yourself. After that happened, I wanted to be a goal scorer and be a difference-maker. Suddenly, I was doing that, then producing points, playing on the penalty kill and power play, and trying to be the best player I could be on all my teams. As I was hitting my goals, I never thought about playing 1,000 games or scoring 500 goals, but as you get closer to those numbers, you do find yourself using them as motivation. For me, my biggest goal in hockey obviously became to win a Stanley Cup. It's what drove me for many years. I was lucky enough to win the Stanley Cup three times and play in the Stanley Cup Final five times. To win those Stanley Cups with the Blackhawks and reach all those other career milestones was just proof I had made the right decision to sign with them all those years back. I had gone with my gut and it had been right.

Nine

I never saw Raffi Torres coming.

I was normally able to avoid injuries when taking a hit. I read the ice well and was always prepared for something like that. As soon as I stepped foot off the bench, I could envision how things would play out. I was normally able to see a hit coming and put myself in the best position to absorb it. But when we were playing the Phoenix Coyotes in the Western Conference quarterfinals at the United Center in Chicago in 2012, I never saw Torres, which meant I wasn't prepared for him to hit me like he did.

The play happened about midway through the first period. I won the puck near our bench and began skating up ice. I passed it and was going to the bench. Torres was behind me. It all happened in a split second. I was turning to change and definitely wasn't expecting to be hit. When you're not prepared for it, that's the worst thing. You can't deflect. Your body is loose. When someone is coming at you at that speed, too, it's like being hit by a truck. I had never been hit that hard in my life.

I was out cold. I don't think I was out long, maybe a few seconds. I woke up laying on the ice. I wasn't exactly in pain. It wasn't anything like the pain I felt when I tore my ACL. This was more like I was just sleepy. I felt funny. Something wasn't right, but I also realized I was going to be OK when they put me on the stretcher. Then I thought about my wife and her watching what just happened at home. I stuck my thumb up while on the stretcher to let her know I was going to be OK.

In the hallway of the United Center, Mike Terry, the Blackhawks doctor, came up to the stretcher. He asked if any of my family was home in Chicago. I told him, yeah, my wife's home. At least, I *thought* she was at home. But she wasn't there and hadn't been watching the game live. She had left a few days earlier to go back home to Slovakia. Mike Terry knew that, too, so he must have known right away something wasn't right with me. After that, I fell asleep and woke up in an ambulance, and there was Blackhawks president John McDonough sitting next to me. I'm lying there, I open my eyes, and John McDonough is beside me. I felt like I was dreaming. Like, what is John McDonough doing in the ambulance? I started to get my mind together after a few moments.

I thought, I got hit hard, but why would John McDonough be in the ambulance with me? But it was a nice gesture by him. He was worried, so he came downstairs and went with me to the hospital.

At that point, I still didn't know who hit me. After I arrived at the hospital, I slowly started putting everything together. But when I was laying on the ice and later in the ambulance going to the hospital, I didn't know it was Torres who hit me. I did end up watching the hit later. I watched it many times. There were the highlights of it on TV and you could find it on the internet. I was able to see all the different angles and look at it over and over. I wanted to make sure it wasn't my mistake that got me hit like that. You make that same play so many times. You play the puck, look, pass it, and then turn around to change. I obviously could have gotten hit doing that many times, but players usually respect you in that space. I knew it was the playoffs and it's more intense, but you still don't anticipate being hit there. As I discovered, he was obviously late with the hit, and he would later be suspended for it.

I suffered a concussion. When I went home that first night, our trainer, Jeff Thomas, came with me. He knew I was going home alone, with my family being in Slovakia. He was always really good to me. We had a great relationship. He would do anything for me and deserves a lot of credit. I appreciated him staying with me that night. He slept in the other room and made sure to check on me. He told me the next morning his bedroom was really cold, but he didn't want to wake me. I then showed him the thermostat in the room. We laughed about it.

I stayed home for I don't know how many days. I couldn't go anywhere. Noises bugged me at the beginning. Lights would bother me and forced me to close the curtains. It was like nothing I felt before. I had been hit hard and you sometimes wouldn't feel great afterward, but it was nothing like this. This was by far the most impactful hit I had taken. I had teammates calling me. Joel Quenneville called me. People from the front office called. Teammate Andrew Brunette came over to my place to check on me. He crushed a few beers and we had a good talk about everything. He is a great guy and I've always enjoyed his sense of humor.

Everyone just wanted to make sure I was doing OK. They wanted to know if I needed anything because they knew I was home alone. I don't even know if I watched the playoff game after that. We ended up losing the series in six games. That year, the Coyotes were the better team and they beat us. Thank God I started feeling better, though.

A few days after the hit, Torres called me. One of the PR guys said Raffi wanted to call me and asked if it was OK. I was like, yeah, sure. I wasn't going to be some asshole and say, no. So, he called. He said, "Just sorry hitting you late. Maybe it

Dad teaching Marcel and me the basics of hockey

That's me sitting in the front row wearing the C for Dukla Trenčín's junior team

At home with my mom, Mária

Marty Havlát celebrates his game-winning goal against the Flyers with me and Radek Bonk in the playoffs in 2002. The three of us also hung out a lot together off the ice. *(Getty Images)*

On the ice with Marcel, when he was with the Rangers and I was with Atlanta. My brother had a great career: he played in 250-plus NHL games, led the KHL scoring for a season, and played on our national team and in the Olympics. *(Getty Images)*

With Sidney Crosby in the Bahamas after the 2008 season. I didn't play with Sid for a long time, but he'll always be one of my favorite teammates.

On the ice with my parents in Boston after winning our second Stanley Cup

At our wedding in Slovakia in 2010. Even though we almost forgot her dress in Chicago, Jana looked stunning.

Stan Mikita (left), Peter Bondra (above), and I are the only Slovakian players to score 500 career NHL goals, and Stan, Peter Šťastný (below), and I are the only three Slovakians in the Hockey Hall of Fame.

Three Stanley Cup winners on one street: Big Z, me, and Gabby

After scoring two goals in 17 seconds against Boston, we hit the ice to celebrate winning our second Stanley Cup in 2013. *(Getty Images)*

Another champagne shower for Joel Quenneville after winning our second Stanley Cup against the Bruins in 2013. *(Getty Images)*

With Jana's parents and the Stanley Cup in 2013

Tazer and I in the dressing room before the Winter Classic practice in 2014 *(Getty Images)*

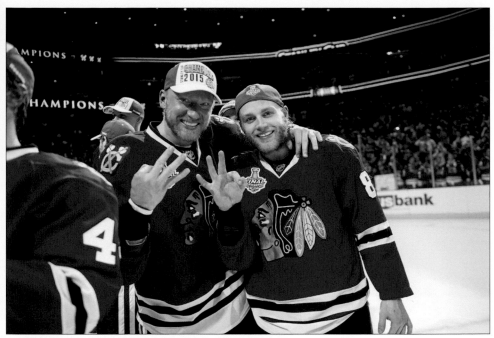

In 2015, Patrick Kane and I won our third Cup together with the Blackhawks

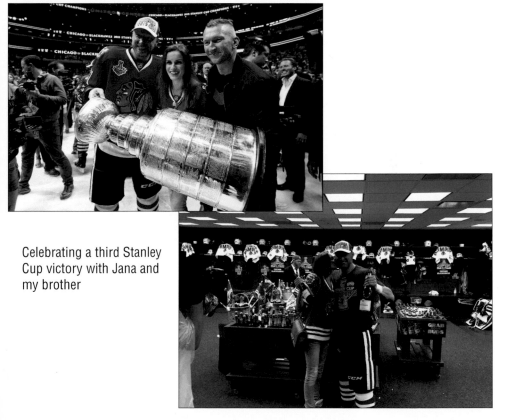

Celebrating a third Stanley Cup victory with Jana and my brother

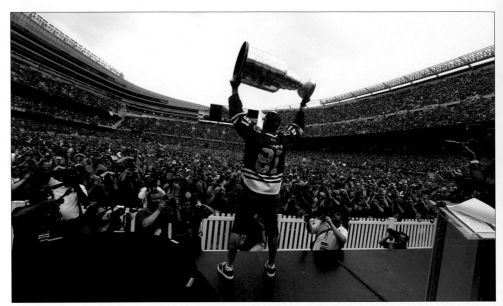

Being able to celebrate before our home fans at Soldier Field was amazing that third time. Blackhawks fans were great throughout my career.

My dad and I taking Lord Stanley's Cup for a dip in my parents' pool

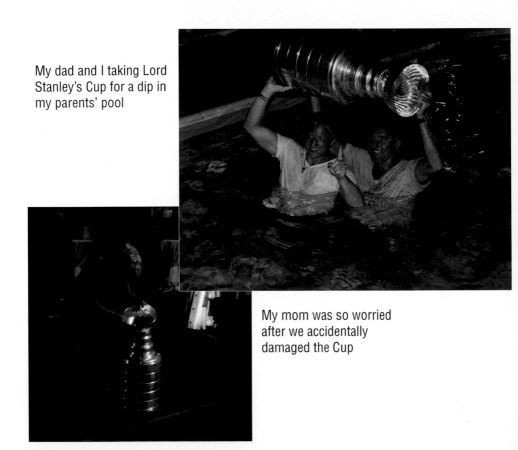

My mom was so worried after we accidentally damaged the Cup

Marián Gáborík, Pavol Demitra, and I celebrating Gabby's goal against Finland at the Olympics in 2010 *(AP Images)*

The Blackhawks had a big ceremony at the United Center to commemorate my 500 career goals

Nothing is more important to me than family. It is always special to spend time with Jana and the girls, whether we're in the Alps, Cabo, Mexico, meeting Santa Claus, or in the dressing room.

My friends Rasty, Big Pete, Lemon and I at the World Championship in Bratislava in 2019.

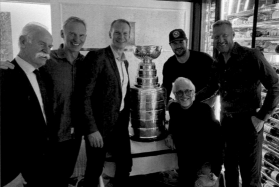

Clockwise: Former Senators GM Marshall Johnston and his wife, Barbara, with my parents at my Hockey Hall of Fame dinner. Marshall was the man who drafted me back in 1997; With Lanny McDonald, Dominik Hašek, Nicklas Lidström, Brent Seabrook, and Ritch Winter at my Hockey Hall of Fame dinner; With my former Winterhawks coaches Brent Peterson and Július Šupler

With my family and Lanny McDonald before the Hockey Hall of Fame ceremony at Scotiabank Centre in Toronto

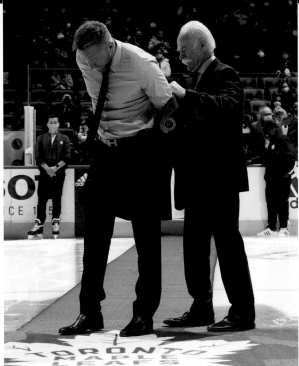

Slipping on my Hockey Hall of Fame jacket during the ceremony

I have been lucky to share so many good times with family and friends, including at Jeremy Bieber's wedding in Jamaica and after we won our third Cup in Chicago.

I asked Nick Lidström to introduce me at the Hockey Hall of Fame induction. He was a role model for me on and off the ice.

On the plane home from Toronto after my induction. We had to wait for the actual ceremony, due to COVID, but it was worth it.

wasn't right, but that's my style of game. I didn't want to hurt you." Obviously, he apologized to me. I told him, well, thanks for calling. Obviously I've never gotten hit so hard, and, hopefully, I'll be OK and will recover. He did get a significant suspension for the hit, and he said he's going to have a lot of time to work on his skills instead of, you know, violence. It was a pretty quick conversation. But I told him, thanks for calling. What else am I going to say? I did also say to him, I hope you learn from it because that's another suspension for you. You could hurt somebody or do something even worse, and I'm sure you don't want that. I know that's your style of game, but on the other hand, you have to be responsible. I was obviously angry in the beginning. But then time went on, and it's not like you can change anything. I actually never realized how angry Blackhawks fans were at him. I was in a fog for some time and didn't follow any of that in the days after.

I was worried about my future at first following the hit. I was still at the beginning of my contract with the Blackhawks. I had so much more I wanted to accomplish there. But I started feeling better with time. After we lost the series, I went home to Slovakia and began to relax. I went to see a doctor in Slovakia for the concussion. I started rehab to help clear my mind and I could tell I was beginning to make progress. I stopped worrying, at least as much as I had been. I felt like I was heading in the right direction.

That offseason led into the NHL lockout. I talked to Stan
Bowman before the lockout because no one was sure what
was going to happen. He called me and asked me how I felt.
I told him, I definitely felt better, but I didn't know for sure
where my health was. I didn't know if I was 100 percent yet
or if I would be able to play if the season started. I needed
to be tested more. He said I should come to Chicago early. I
did and rehabbed with the trainers there. I was also skating
again. Other players couldn't get on the ice with the team
staff because of the lockout, but injured players could. There
were a couple of injured guys who were skating with me then.
I also did one tough practice with Troy Murray, a former
NHL player and our radio broadcaster, and Norm Maciver, a
former player who was in the Blackhawks front office. It was a
fun practice with those two guys. They played by the old rules
of hacking and whacking. It took me longer than usual to get
back up to speed once I returned to the ice. But it was good to
have that extra time. Thankfully, my symptoms continued to
fade away and I was ready to return when the season finally
began in January.

When we played the Coyotes and Torres that next season,
Jamal Mayers came up to me and told me before, "Don't
worry about it, I'll take care of him." Jammer knew I wasn't
going to fight Torres. I'd probably get another concussion
right away. These days, now that I've taken up boxing, maybe

Nine

it'd be different. But it was a really nice gesture by Jammer. He dropped the gloves for me in that first game against the Coyotes in their building. I tried to focus on my game from the start of it. I knew something was going to happen. Torres knew he wasn't going to fight me, but that somebody was going to try to send a message, and Jammer was the guy who did that. It was a nice gesture from a teammate to step up. After the game, I thanked Jammer. I told him I appreciated that.

From that point, I moved on. It was over for me.

Ten

'll never forget the argument Patrick Kane and Jonathan Toews were having during my first season with the Blackhawks. I got back to the bench after a shift, and they were yelling at each other. I was right in the middle of them. Jonny was like, "Kaner, pass the puck." Kaner's like, "What do you mean, pass the puck? You pass the puck." And Jonny's like, "No, you're supposed to pass the puck." I felt like I was at a tennis match with it going back and forth, and I was in the middle. I was like, hold on, guys. This is hilarious. What are you guys talking about? You should hear yourselves. They were like two kids. It was funny, though, because they were two kids who really wanted to do their best and they'd get into it like that. After I enjoyed it for a bit, I told them, OK, guys, you have to stop this because this isn't a junior team.

I had played against Kaner and Jonny in the playoffs the year before when I was with the Red Wings. We were the better team, but you could tell Chicago was young and hungry. They felt like they had something to prove. I could tell the Blackhawks had some superstars coming and would have a really solid core for a long time. As I was making my decision where to sign that offseason, knowing I would be playing with those two players for a long time definitely helped in my decision to join the Blackhawks for 12 years.

Having played with Sid in Pittsburgh, there were certain similarities coming to Chicago to play with Jonny. Everyone's a little different, but they had some common traits. Both were named captains at an early age. You could see why with both of them. Not everyone can handle that, but they handled that extremely well. They also had a lot of success, whether it was in the NHL or on the Canadian national team. I always thought, these two guys are born leaders. Jonny was exactly like Sid in that he was vocal but not too vocal, worked hard, and wanted to play hockey the right way.

Jonny and I clicked early on too. He's such a nice guy. He asked me questions about certain things, but we didn't necessarily talk a lot in the beginning. But after we started playing together, we became better friends. We definitely clicked on the ice right away. We were two talented guys who were playing the game the right way. It's tough to play against

Jonny because he comes back and takes care of his own zone first. That's how I was playing the game then too. If you have a couple of two-way players on the same line, that's not easy to play against. We were responsible defensively, but we also had some offensive threat. Jonny definitely liked when others were working just as hard as he was. I had talent, could make plays and score goals, but if you were willing to work hard, he'd do the same. That's what he was looking for, because he thought talent wasn't good enough. He wanted our line to work hard. He loved that. I never had a problem with that either and that's the reason why we clicked.

We also played together for a long time. We became closer on and off the ice, but we also realized we couldn't stop working hard no matter what. We didn't give each other breaks. We knew we'd be cheating each other and the team if we did, and our play would suffer. I think our mentality was always to be the best we could possibly be. We also knew we were the leaders and the other guys were looking at us. We couldn't take shortcuts or they'd follow us. If they saw us playing hard shift after shift, maybe they would too. It helped that we had so many other leaders on the team. But I really liked playing with Jonny and I got to know him better than a lot of my centermen in my career. We had a lot of fun together.

With Kaner, we didn't play as much together. I did sit next to him in the locker room for nearly my entire time in Chicago.

There was also the one season where we were linemates when Joel decided to put Kaner at center as an experiment. We had a lot of fun because he's such a creative player. We'd have give-and-gos. He'd come pick up the puck, use his speed, and I'd try to match his speed and travel in the same wave as him. Even if I was skating behind him, he could stop, pass me the puck, and I'd have that speed going. He created a lot even though he wasn't a natural-born center. It was amazing. He learned how to play center really quickly. We tried to help him down low. We knew if we took care of our zone, we'd get lots of possibilities to create offensively.

In the locker room, Kaner was in one stall, there was an empty stall between us, and then there was me. We were in the corner and enjoyed having a little extra space. We had so much fun together there. It was nice to sit beside him because we could talk about certain plays between periods. He just loves hockey too. He told me a story about when he was a little kid his dad took him to a lot of NHL games and he could remember the tape job of my stick and how I only had two stripes. I was like, really? It was funny because I could remember when I was younger and I would notice those things about players I liked. I felt like when I came into the league I knew everyone's lineups and how the star players taped their sticks. With Kaner, I saw someone who really liked hockey because not everybody will tell you how a certain player tapes their stick. You have to really be into it, and you could tell how excited and hungry he was to be in the NHL. He'd ask me about older players too. We had a lot of fun sitting next to each other.

My first impression of him was how super talented he was. He didn't care about much of anything else other than playing and winning. He's always having fun on the ice, not just winning. He's an entertainer. People come to watch the Blackhawks especially because of Patrick Kane and the things he does. He surprises fans and brings them out of their seats. When I wasn't playing with him, I had a really good seat to watch him make plays. And then in the dressing room, we'd talk about those plays.

One of my favorite Kane stories occurred while we were both training one day while injured. We were working out when someone from the Los Angeles Lakers staff came in and asked if one of their players could train there as well. They were playing the Bulls that night. We were like, sure. In walks Kobe Bryant. Kobe said, "What's up, guys?" Kaner and I just looked at each other. We were about finished in the gym, but we stuck around to watch him a bit. We tried not to stare. It was special to see him up close. I should have told Kobe about the signed jersey I had of his hanging up in my office, but I was so stunned that it was actually him. Back when I was with Ottawa, our president/CEO at the time, Roy

Mlakar, would brag he had a connection with Kobe and could get me an autographed jersey. I took him up on it, thinking he wouldn't come through. Well, one day he showed up with a signed jersey and a personalized picture from Kobe. I was stunned and at the same time thankful for a super gift. Kaner came away with an even better story: he went to the basketball game that evening and was sitting pretty close to the court. Kobe saw him and gave him a nod.

Kane and Toews were kind enough to share their memories of playing with me with Scott.

Jonathan Toews

Marián was one of those guys I watched when I was a teenager. I always had a hard time picking my favorite team and I always kind of had my favorite players. Like, I loved Joe Sakic for a lot of years, the Avalanche were a favorite team of mine. But every year I was kind of crushed because I always wanted to see a Canadian team do well in the playoffs, and I always thought Ottawa had the best chance to do that, because to me, they seemed like the best team. I remember seeing all these skilled lefties like Antoine Vermette and Marián Hossa and Martin Havlát, you know, Daniel Alfredsson, all these guys. They were so fun to watch and they would just get absolutely... like, it was just like prison rules against the Maple Leafs every year.

So I remember just watching him and how smooth he was. He was like a big Marián Gáborík and big Pavel Bure, who could just fly, and he was so smooth and lit it up obviously in Atlanta.

Once he got to Detroit, that team was a powerhouse. There's no reason why they shouldn't have won two in a row there. I remember those games we had my rookie season where we actually snuck up on them and got a bunch of wins. I think we won like five of eight my rookie season against Detroit. That really fired up the Chicago Blackhawks fans. But when he was there, it was like they were this unstoppable powerhouse, and we were almost kind of in awe of them. We were in a shootout one time, and I forget, it might have been Zetterberg, Datsyuk, Hossa, and they all come down and score. Hossa came down and I'd never seen him do this before, though obviously I saw him do it quite a bit after that, but he came down and took a full slap shot on a shootout and went absolute top shelf. I don't even think he hit the post. He fit it in exactly. And I was like, OK, how are we going to match that? He was this big guy, raw talent, so smooth, and so fun to watch. So you play against him, you definitely have respect, but you almost enjoy just watching him too. So yeah, he was a special player to watch before I ever got the chance to play with him.

I never remember being part of a specific plan, and nothing was ever said to me that we'd play together. I think my first couple of years I was used to playing with Kaner a lot and whoever else kind of fit in there. As time went along, the fact that we had some guys that can score in our lineup, Hoss didn't have to be that 90-point guy, 100-point guy, he could just be a depth guy, and that made our team so much more dangerous. I think it helped in a lot of ways to split up Kaner and I. Hossa and I complemented each other in that role immensely, where we were able to go toe to toe with top lines every day and keep them in their zone. And he was such a heady player and such a hard player to play against. One of those guys that can hang on to the puck. I would get mad at him when I wanted the puck and he could take two, three guys on his back and still hang on and eventually make a play. But I mean, that's why he was so difficult to play against. You couldn't take the puck off him. Then when things are going back towards our end, I was down low in the offensive zone all the time, so I relied upon him so much to get back there. All those years, we had a lot of very high plus-minus years where we didn't spend much time on our end, if at all.

I think when you put great players together, it's probably more rare than not that you can just go out there and make things happen on raw talent. But there's no doubt that if you have different games and differ-ent mindsets, and you're able to kind of talk it out and figure things out with each other, there's no doubt that chemistry is going to build over time. And you know, we definitely had that for sure.

It's easy to be intimidated by older guys that have the history and the ability and the career that he had before he came in, but it didn't take long. It was easy to look up to him. He was never imposing in any way. I think he led by example, and he was naturally himself

162

and you felt very comfortable as a person around him. He's definitely a guy that was easy to become friends with and become close
to, because he was very secure in his ability and his talents and he
was just a natural, down-to-earth guy off the ice. I definitely enjoyed
going to dinners with him and hanging out with him on the road. He's
a guy I constantly looked up to.

He has such a humble nature. Again, talking about his natural
talent and all the things that come with that, it's easy to let that go
to your head. One thing we respected most about Hoss—everyone
talks about, oh, man, he was this and that, and he can do incredible
things with the puck and score highlight-reel goals—was how hard
he backchecks. Sometimes simple things like that really stand out
and are a pretty huge example of a guy's personality. He had that
inner competitive drive, but he wasn't going to show it outwardly.
You just knew it was there. That humility showed that he's just an
approachable person, and I think in a lot of ways showed why he was
such a good leader in our locker room. I don't think he got a whole
lot of credit, kind of like a guy like Hammer, who never got credit for
being key leaders in our core group for all those Stanley Cups, but
there's no doubt that those guys brought so much to the table.

I'll be completely honest, I had no clue how close we were to
winning a Stanley Cup when he arrived. I had no clue what we were
walking into, and I was very caught up in my own process and what
I needed to do to get better as a player and how to lead by example,
and how to learn as a young captain. The more I look back on it, I

realize how much I was actually biting off and trying to chew. So, yeah, when Marián Hossa gets thrown into your lineup, and you just went to the conference finals, you're feeling pretty good. We had some young guys that are coming along, and there were guys in the room like John Madden and Andrew Ladd, who kind of kept whispering we're a little bit naive, we don't really realize how good we are. It's maybe good to a certain degree. But it's good to acknowledge that this is a hell of an opportunity, we need to be pretty cognizant of it. So yeah, when a guy like Marián Hossa gets brought in, it adds a lot of confidence.

I thought I told Marián about handing him the Cup first [in 2010] when we were skating around for morning skate, but he could be right. I didn't feel like I was jinxing it at all because I'm like, that's a pretty important detail and not really going to change the course of whether we're supposed to win this thing or not. So I had asked Sharpie and Duncs if that was OK, and they're like, yeah, absolutely. It was one of those things that popped in my head and felt pretty important in the moment. I'm like, yeah, that feels right, I'm just gonna kind of go with that feeling, and I felt confident we're gonna get the job done. So pretty cool moment for me as a captain to win a Stanley Cup and hand it off to a guy like him. He's the Slovakian rock star hero. Like him and his brother, Marcel Hossa, they knew how to party, and I'm sure he learned a thing or two from his little brother over the years on how to burn the midnight oil.

I learned a lot from Hoss but he was pretty easy for me to learn from. I don't know if I was as easy on [Brandon Saad]. You can ask Saader that, probably he'll tell you that he wanted to pull his hair out a time or two playing with me. Saader had a big body, could skate, and fit that up-and-down, two-way game that we were playing. He grew into a really high-level star player so much faster than I thought he ever would too. It was amazing to see. He made that line a lot better. The three of us had a similar mix of all those skills. We all seemed to make plays, score goals, play defense, and all those things, so we had a pretty good balance there.

On the bench, it was usually just me yapping and Hoss telling me to calm down because he was just centered. He was calm. It was unemotional and it was rare when you'd see him get angry or pissed off or frustrated. But you knew that if he did, he was really fired up. We liked to talk about things that were happening and discuss plays. I just did it habitually sometimes. That bothered guys even if it wasn't coming from a bad place, you know, but Hoss didn't seem to mind for the most part. Put me in my place a few times, no doubt.

I knew quite a bit about his skin condition. But you're not a doctor, so you don't really know. You try to be helpful. We all heard about Bryan Bickell, who went through MS, and I'm sure that hurt his career in a lot of ways before he even became aware of it. As hockey players, we put our bodies through so much stress even though everyone thinks we're healthy all the time. Maybe in some ways it was his body telling him it was a good way to call it a career and say, hey, things have gone incredibly well, don't push your luck. It sounds like he's doing really well right now, so it's good to hear.

There was some public kind of accusation of him, or people who thought the Blackhawks were trying to pull tricks for the cap or something. But there's no doubt he was going through a lot. I remember the World Cup year where he could hardly [play]. You know he was in a lot of pain because he had those skin rashes and those reactions everywhere. When he put that equipment on, it was just automatic. It was like some kind of immune or skin reaction, so it was really difficult. Probably confusing for a long time, but I knew enough that he was going through a lot and he was pretty frustrated. He was in pain. So it's a weird thing for some people to maybe judge you for it. But as far as I'm concerned, he wanted to keep playing. He had more in the tank. But this is something that was kind of steering him in a direction where he had to accept it. And maybe I'm wrong in saying that, maybe those aren't his words, but I think it was a lot for him to deal with.

It was a massive, massive void that he left behind. You don't realize how much the culture of the locker room doesn't just depend on two guys. You can't be in the training room, you can't be in the gym, you can't be in the locker room all at once. You need different guys with different personalities that understand the winning culture of your locker room. It goes beyond anything that he ever did on the ice, which says a lot. When a guy like that just disappears overnight, it leaves a pretty huge hole that you're starting to wonder how to fix it. Losing a guy like him, it's almost an easy equation. It's easy to say that we haven't quite recovered as a team from having Marián Hossa be a part of our Stanley Cup run.

It's kind of crazy to think of how long he's been gone already. Time really does fly. But he's always a guy who is easy to talk to. It's fun to catch up with him and see what his life's looking like back in Trenčín now. His girls are growing up and life's different. But for the most part, we're getting the old Instagram updates on the next ski trip or Hawaii trip with the family. Yeah, Hoss doesn't seem to mind retirement. I think he knows how to live his best life at all times.

Patrick Kane

I grew up going to Sabres games, and I remember watching Hossa when he was on Ottawa, and he always seemed to score against the Sabres. He was a great skater. He had a really unique tape job back then, where he had two or three strands of tape just like the tone of his stick, and that was it. Obviously when he went to Atlanta, he was good there with Kovalchuk. And when he was in Pittsburgh, in Detroit, he was always a guy that I liked to watch. Especially that year in Detroit, he was so special with Datsyuk, had three assists against us in the Winter Classic that year. He was obviously a guy that was gonna be a big, sought-after free agent. There were rumblings that maybe we would be able to pursue someone like that. He was my winger a lot when I was playing center that one season, and he made life so easy for me. I wish maybe my production was a little bit better, but there were games we played together when we had chance after chance and a lot of nice plays off the rush. I look at that as a successful experiment, but I think if I didn't have him, it probably would have been a lot harder.

The spin-o-rama was a nice play with him. Sometimes we got out there four-on-four and he'd come up to me and say, "I give you the puck, spin-o-rama, and I'm going to the back post." He would always beat his guy to the back post, that's one thing you can count on. I always liked setting him up for the one-timer because he had a really good one-timer. His shootout slap shot was pretty cool. He had a pretty flexible stick. You'd see the replay and you'd see how much the stick was flexing. If you're a goalie, what are you supposed to do? A guy comes in and shoots a slap shot that hard, hits his spot, it's pretty much impossible to stop.

A lot of us looked up to how professional he was and how he took care of himself. We would always joke around if he missed games or was injured or took a day or two off from practice because he needed rest, because he always seemed to come back and be the best guy on the ice no matter how much time he took off. He seemed to have a perfect hockey body. He was tall, he was very strong but not overly big, and had that long stride, so just like a perfect, all-around hockey player.

He and Tazer were very strong on the puck. It seemed like no one could really take the puck off those two, especially when they were in the offensive zone. And then obviously add in the skill factor, they were both able to make plays. Both of them were so good defensively back then. They made it pretty much impossible for teams to play. They were so strong offensively, they're so competitive defensively, taking pucks away, winning battles, and heading the other way again. So it made for a tough line to play against, no doubt.

Everyone knows him as a classy guy, but I feel like he was always in a good mood. Some days I'd be a little bit grumpy or whatever it may be, but he always seemed to be in a good mood. Nothing really ever seemed to throw it off. He was always fun to sit next to, fun to talk to about hockey, but also fun to kind of joke around with and laugh about certain things, kind of whatever was going on that day, but never really a dull moment. It was always refreshing coming to the rink and knowing that you're gonna be by him and be close to him throughout the whole season and throughout the day. He was fun to be around. I sat next to [Andrew Shaw] for a little bit—we kind of switched around the locker room—and sometimes you had to tell him to kind of be quiet. But with Hossa, he was always fun to be around. I think I sat next to him for maybe six or seven years, and there was really never a time where I was like, oh, I need to get away from this guy and next to someone else. That thought never crossed your mind.

There was one time we were sitting next each other and we were watching Rozy [Michal Rozsíval] getting ready for practice, and he didn't have the steel part into his skates. We were just watching and we didn't know if we should like tell him. So we're kind of laughing together and, sure enough, Rozy goes out there without the steel in his skates and falls and started blaming the equipment manager. So we always got a kick out of that, pretty much every day after that, we'll be checking on Rozy to see if he had the steel on and laugh about that.

He was very funny, too, and I feel like that's one of the things that maybe doesn't get talked about him too much. But if you kind of went at him a little bit, he was very witty. We were in Dallas one time and there were a lot of pranks going on at that point. I think Sharpie and Burish did something. I can't really remember. But Hossa texted me that night, like, what are you doing for dinner? And I was like, oh, going with Sharp and Burish, and then I didn't really hear from him. Sure enough, we come back and we're just kind of hanging out in the room. They start like feeling around their beds after like 15 minutes, and sure enough their beds are just soaked with water. It was funny because it was completely soaked, but he put the sheets back up perfectly so you wouldn't really notice.

I think now I realize the biggest thing is how much he meant to our team. Ever since he's been gone, our team hasn't made the playoffs, except that bubble year in there. I know he ended up playing more on the third line his last year, but that's a guy you can put anywhere in the lineup and it looks good. He was a top line player in my mind. Obviously when you look at him and Tazer on the first line, and then I was on the second line, it made my life a lot easier as far as the pressure to produce and probably having easier matchups. But just really what he meant to our team and his presence around the locker room the way he played the game, it was something everyone could look up to.

I saw what he was going through with his skin every day. I remember one day he came in the locker room and they were trying different fabrics to see what could help. Most guys wear dark underwear under their equipment and he came in wearing all white, so he looked like a white knight, and we all kind of laughed. But it was tough on him. He didn't really practice much those last years with us. It seemed like they were going through a lot of trial and error to see what would work. And I guess the one thing that actually worked wasn't so good for his body, so it was pretty unfortunate. You could see he was trying to figure out things every day, so I'm sure that was tough. I know how good of a player he still was, so it was surprising from that sense when he stopped playing. But when you sit back and think about it, you have your life after hockey and your future to consider. I think myself and a lot of us kind of understood the decision.

We text each other every now and then. It was nice to see him when we went over to Prague and played over there. It's always fun to hear from him. He's such a classy guy. He'll text me and reach out to me if there's a nice play or I reach a certain milestone. He always seems to be on top of that stuff.

Eleven

One of the perks of winning the Stanley Cup three times was getting to know the Cup keepers. They would travel to Trenčín each time and spend a few days with my family, friends, and me along with the Cup. Through that, there was some trust built up. So in 2015, during my third go-around with the Stanley Cup, I asked for a favor. Normally, the keepers would take the Cup home late into the night. It was officially the end of the Cup day for that player.

But this time, I asked if I could keep the Stanley Cup overnight. We were in the garden at my parents' house and having a good time with some close friends and family. It wasn't anything out of control. I told the Cup keepers I'd sleep with it there and that nothing would happen to it. They did seem to really like my family and friends. They spent time with my grandpa. He didn't speak a word of English, but they found a way to communicate, and he was telling them stories. Plus, the keepers were pretty tired. I reminded them the Cup had been fine the first two times I had it. Nothing had happened then, and nothing would happen now. They finally agreed.

Everything was fine, until about 2 or 3 a.m. The Cup was in the middle of the dance floor, and my cousin started jumping over it. The DJ was playing a Slovak song where the lyrics included jumping higher and higher. Everyone was getting into it. A lot of people jumped over it easily. But then one person—who I have promised never to reveal—didn't clear it. He jumped and landed with his full weight, butt first, on top of the Cup. He hopped off the Cup and you could immediately see it was tilted. He would soon have a significant bruise on his butt too. The Cup looked like a sunflower. I have the video on my phone. Everyone was like, shit. Then we started laughing because everyone was drunk. My mom was so worried. She was like, what now?

We tried to force the Cup back into shape, but it wasn't moving. We were all so drunk, which obviously didn't help. A few of my buddies decided they would try to fix it. They hadn't fixed anything in their lives and all of a sudden they're going to fix the Stanley Cup? I'm like, OK, guys, let's give it a try, gently. We got a rubber hammer and put a towel over the Cup to soften the blow. We didn't want to permanently damage it. We were knocking it in hopes of putting it back into place, but it wasn't budging. It was impossible. I was like, what am I going to tell them tomorrow when they come pick up the Cup? I was getting worried, but I was also laughing.

We ended up hammering it back into place somewhat. You could see it was better than it had been, but it wasn't perfect. It was around 4 a.m. at that point. Everybody wanted to know what I was going to tell the Cup keepers in the morning. I didn't know. I thought I'd think of something in the morning. I went to sleep.

That next morning I saw their VW pulling up in my driveway. I was scratching my head. What am I going to tell them? The two keepers of the Cup were in the backseat of the car with their seatbelts on. I walked up and I said, "Hey, guys, what's up?" They asked if I had a good time and if everything was OK. I was like, "Um…" As soon as they heard the hesitation, I heard "click, click." They had undone their seatbelts and were getting out. They're like, "OK, tell us what happened." I had to lie because I didn't want them to know we were jumping over the Cup. I said I was going up the stairs to bed, tripped, and the Cup came down the stairs, and the fall had bent it a little bit. They asked how bad it was. I said, well, it's not great, but it's not all bad. They went to look, and I could see it in their faces. They were like, fuck. They were expecting for it to be worse in some ways, but they saw it was definitely damaged. I told them, "I'm sorry, guys, it shouldn't have happened, but it fell down the stairs. It was an accident." I said I was embarrassed because they had trusted me and nothing like that had happened the two times before. I had to lie, right? I couldn't tell them someone had damaged the Stanley Cup trying to leap over it.

I told the keepers I knew someone who had a garage and could possibly fix it. He was a handyman, a father of one of my buddies, who lived on my street. We took it to his garage. We kept the garage door closed. We didn't want anyone to see what we were doing. He turned the lights on, and he started unscrewing the Stanley Cup piece by piece. The keepers of the Cup were like, "OK, guys, nobody can take any pictures, nobody can take videos. This can't go anywhere." My buddy Johny and my friend's father were able to make it better. It wasn't perfect by any means, but it was definitely better.

I still had another day with the Cup. We had a party planned at the Trenčín castle, Trenčiansky hrad, that night. We ended up turning the Cup around, so people couldn't see the slightly damaged side and could still take pictures with it. The Cup keepers were probably disappointed in me because I was the one they trusted to not damage it. But I don't think they were totally upset. It did provide a valuable lesson: they shouldn't trust anyone with the Cup overnight. My friends and I probably ruined that for every player from there on. The Stanley Cup would definitely be taken home at midnight regardless of anyone's pleas. That was best for everyone and especially the Cup.

The Cup's next stop was with defenseman Michal Rozsíval in the Czech Republic. After it arrived, I got a text message from him later that day. He wrote me, "Holy shit, Hoss, what did you do with the Cup?" I'm like, why? He's like, "It's tilted sideways." I wrote back, "I think you're drinking too much. You're not seeing it correctly."

We kept what happened pretty quiet after that. The next season, the first question everybody in the Blackhawks locker room had for me was, "Hoss, what happened to the Cup?" I said, "What can I tell you? It bounced down the stairs."

Twelve

I first started noticing something wasn't right with my skin during the 2013 Stanley Cup playoffs. It had been game, practice, game, practice, for two months. My skin didn't get a chance to breathe because I was sweating and wearing the equipment so much. Over time, it got much worse.

Not to gross you out, but what would happen is there would be pus leaking from my skin if it didn't have enough time to breathe. The pus was a yellowish color. It was ugly and more so it made me uncomfortable. After the pus dried, my skin would blister. Those blisters itched and then I began scratching them and then there was blood. It was a frustrating cycle. I was embarrassed by what the hotel housekeepers must have thought of me when cleaning up my bed. They must have thought some pig had stayed there. Sometimes my jeans would get all wet in certain spots from my skin leaking. It was disgusting.

We tried so many different things to help it. I went to the doctor to see if I was allergic to something. They placed sensors on my body that I had to keep on for a few days and couldn't practice with. They thought maybe it was the fabric that was affecting me, like the latex. They had me try different brands of materials under my equipment. Someone mentioned I shouldn't use any colored material, so I started wearing all white—white socks, white underwear, everything. Some guys in the locker room were making jokes about it, but I didn't really care, I laughed too. The trainers were trying

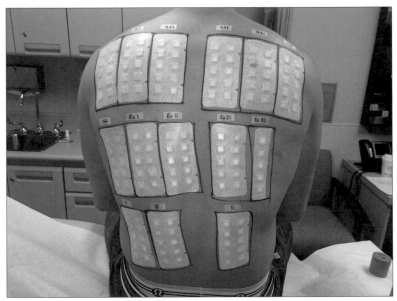

One of the many tests we did to try and help the condition of my skin

all sorts of things. They tried different soap. They washed my clothes and equipment separately from everyone else's. They gave me new equipment. They gave me some cortisone creams and stuff like that. We tried it all. We managed it for a few years and then it got worse and worse.

It really hit me during the World Cup of Hockey in Toronto when I was playing for Team Europe in 2016. I arrived to the team all clean and healed up from the summer. I was fine and then we started practicing and I started seeing the issues again. The equipment was really irritating my skin worse than ever before. I don't know if it was how they were washing it or what, but there was something that was really bothering it. The tournament hadn't even started. I had different trainers then I usually did, so I had to explain to them about my skin and show I've had this history of rashes. They were trying to keep an eye on it.

As a team, we started winning games and playing well. But while that was happening, my skin was only getting worse. We beat Sweden in the semifinals and everyone was going to dinner. I told them I couldn't and went back to my hotel room. My skin was leaking and it was all over the sheets. I sent a picture to the Blackhawks trainers explaining what was happening. I was really frustrated.

A day later, we had a practice before playing Canada in the championship game. I was showing the team doctors what was happening. I'm like, how am I supposed to go on the ice? They're like, Hoss, you have to do something about this. I wasn't sure how I was going to get through the upcoming NHL season. I wasn't even sure if I was going to play against Canada in the championship game. They ended up wrapping me like a mummy so I wouldn't leak all over. I wasn't going to miss the game, but it was so uncomfortable. I felt bad because those Team Europe trainers weren't used to what I was going through.

We lost to Canada in the final, and then I left for Chicago for the upcoming season. I didn't know it then, but it would be my last in the NHL.

JOEL QUENNEVILLE KNEW all about my condition. He saw me lying there with the trainers in the morning. I said, look at me, guys, I don't want put the equipment on. There were blisters all over my body, leaking and bleeding. It was so uncomfortable. We came up with a plan. If I didn't want to practice, I'd tell them. Joel trusted me. He knew I was going to be in shape, and he knew I wasn't staying away from practice because I didn't *want* to be on the ice. You don't want to miss too many practices, but I had to consider everything else and how my skin was reacting. The upside was, as an older player the extra rest was good for my body. Joel understood I was going to manage myself properly.

Not participating in the morning skates didn't affect me in the games. It might have when I was younger. I enjoyed not having to put the equipment on. The mornings were more relaxed because I would go to the gym or warm up on the bike, just little stuff to get me ready for the game. I knew over the course of my career that morning skates were a bit over-rated. It's great to get into kind of a flow, but then you go back to bed and you're kind of sleepy again. It's good for exercise. But later in my career, I didn't really care about missing them. It was more of a relief. It gave me more jump for the games. I felt more energized later on because I didn't have to go on the ice twice a day. I was mentally ready for the game. We didn't practice the power play much in the morning skate either, so I didn't miss much.

I'm not sure exactly what all my teammates knew. The guys obviously knew I wasn't practicing. Certain guys just don't ask questions. But just based on how my body looked some days, they probably could tell something was wrong. But I didn't talk too much to the guys about it. Everyone has their own problems.

I was able to handle the irritation most of the time, but it was getting more difficult. It was taking a toll on me. The skin condition was affecting me on the ice, but also with my family. My sheets were dirty all the time and my wife was cleaning them. It was just gross. I was sleeping in long underwear. I was sweating. It's the type of stuff no one really cares about, but it was affecting my life and how I lived. I was getting more frustrated. The worst was I had to be careful that my kids didn't touch me in certain spots because of the blisters. I realized I couldn't function like this forever.

I went to see a specialist at some point after I returned from the World Cup. They recommended I try a drug called cyclosporine. I was told if I wanted to stop the rashes and slow the process down, that the pill would help. It did reduce the itching and some of the symptoms. But there were a lot of possible side effects. I had to take two large pills in the morning and two at night. I had a whole section of my drawer devoted to them. I took them throughout the season just to get through it. I had to go to Northwestern Hospital every two weeks to have my blood checked to see how I was reacting to the medication and make sure everything was under control. I told myself I could do it, but I also knew it didn't feel right. You're taking these pills every morning and night. Your wife is telling you, I can't watch you taking those pills. I knew what she meant. I felt the same way about it. I had to get through the season and then we'd have to make a decision on what to do after the season.

The thing is, I was still feeling good on the ice. I felt like I still had my speed and my strength. There weren't a lot of guys who could still beat me in skating, maybe a few, but not many. There was one time we were playing Edmonton and Connor McDavid tried to take the puck away from me and thank God the puck bounced over his stick. When I got back to the bench, I realized he was the first guy I would have no chance to catch. I had never felt that way before. I always felt I could catch everyone or at least I could backcheck and disturb them. But with this guy, I had no chance. I'm like, what the hell just happened?

When we started the playoffs that season, it entered my mind for the first time that I may be playing my last games. I had never gone through a season like that with my condition. My skin was getting beat up. In those playoffs, we got down 3–0 in the first round to the Predators. Nashville was really on fire. When we got to Game 4, I was thinking this could be my last game, my last warmups, and so on. I just couldn't take those pills anymore. We lost that fourth game and got swept.

I remember sitting in the dressing room afterward. It was quiet. Everyone was really down. It hit me that it was likely my last game. I was about 99.9 percent sure of it at that moment. I almost had tears in my eyes. I didn't tell anyone, though. It would have been a weird feeling if I had told anyone then. I kept that to myself. I nearly scored 30 goals that season. I still wanted to play. I felt good and recharged. It was tough going out like that, being swept by Nashville. I thought, this is how I finish my career? There was a lot of stuff going through my

me that. I'm also glad the National Hockey League sent me to a doctor I had never met before. It reassured me I was doing the right thing. I don't think any athlete should have to go through with that with any uncertainty.

I made a lot of phone calls the day it was announced I was leaving hockey because of my skin. I tried to let the people close to me know before it became public. It was still obviously a surprise to a lot of people.

There was a lot of reaction to it. I didn't mind that people began questioning if I left hockey because of how my contract was structured. It probably looked that way to them. But the Blackhawks organization and my family knew exactly what I was struggling with the last couple years of my career. They saw it on a daily basis. The trainers knew for so long and they kept it really quiet. I wasn't surprised that fans and other teams may have reacted as if I was a fraud. I don't blame them for that. But I wouldn't be able to sleep if I was cheating the game like that. Throughout my whole career, I was never known to cheat. If I felt I was able to play, I would have still played those last few seasons.

The Blackhawks wanted to trade my contract after the announcement, but I told them they couldn't. I had a no-movement clause. I told my agent I wanted to end up with the Blackhawks and didn't want to go somewhere else. McDonough called me that summer and I told him how I felt and he respected that, so they didn't trade my contract. Obviously Stan was trying to do his job as GM to improve the team, so I don't blame him either. But I also had my pride, and I wasn't some Joe Schmo in the league. I didn't want to just be a contract ready to be traded.

I wasn't sure how it was going to be for me, having to watch the team and not playing. I knew I was going to be in Chicago. My kids were still attending school there. I went to the team meeting before training camp, like I always did. I asked Stan if I should be there or not. He told me I was going on injured reserve and it wasn't like I was going to be training. He wasn't exactly sure how to answer that, but he thought I probably didn't need to be there.

It was definitely different to be around the team then. Watching the games from the press box was a huge change. You saw the game differently after being on the bench for so many years. I went to the home games. I'd sometimes mention something to the coaches to consider. I didn't do it much, but it was cool they thought about what I said. I wasn't around the players too much either, but they sometimes asked me what I thought.

It was a tough year for the Blackhawks. McDonough called me again after they realized they weren't going to make the playoffs that season. He asked me to go to dinner with him and Rocky Wirtz. We talked about everything—my business, their business, hockey. We had a bottle of red wine and some laughs. They told me they understood how I felt about not wanting my contract traded and about remaining with the Blackhawks. But they thought if they could trade my contract, they could get some younger players to improve the team and get back into the playoffs. They respected whatever my answer would be, but they then asked if I would waive my no-trade clause to be traded to the Arizona Coyotes.

I told them how I felt. I was a Blackhawk and had my most successful years in Chicago. I didn't want to retire as a Coyote. Rocky said after my contract was done, he'd sign me for a day so that I could retire with the Blackhawks. When he said that, I began considering it. We talked and talked and talked and I later spoke to Ritch and told him I was going to help the team. I obviously couldn't help them on the ice, but I could help them by allowing them to trade my contract.

When the trade was announced, even if it wasn't my choice I knew it would help them. I felt like I was leaving the Blackhawks family for a little bit and would hopefully be returning really soon.

It was strange later flying to Arizona and going there to have tests done. I did see Hammer when I was there. I went down to the dressing room and we had a great talk. As I was leaving, I saw some young players waiting in line to talk to the coach and GM. I asked if I could pop in the meetings before them. They were all laughing. I knocked on the door and the general manager, John Chayka, and the head coach saw it was me. They started laughing. I said I was next in line and just wanted to shake their hands on a great season. They enjoyed the joke. They were really nice and congratulated me on my career. It was really short, but we had a good laugh.

THE BLACKHAWKS MEDICAL and training staff knew about my condition more intimately than anybody. I gave Dr. Michael Terry permission to talk to Scott about exactly what I was going through with my skin condition. If you still don't believe me for some reason, maybe you'll believe him.

Dr. Michael Terry

A couple years before he ended up leaving hockey, Marián would get to midseason or later in the season and he'd get what looked like eczema or a rash. At first, we treated that with some topical creams, and it worked. Then he finished the season, and he wouldn't have any difficulty. He'd go away all summer; everything was fine. Then he'd come back, and once he started getting his equipment on, his gear on and playing and practicing, we'd start seeing these things again.

It went from infrequent and easily treated, to more frequent, and then became kind of constant. We would have to go with more and more powerful topical cream, and then that wouldn't work eventually. So we'd have to do different medications, and he was taking steroids on occasion to try to quiet things down. But it was a constant battle for him once it started. It was one of those things where it only went in one direction. The rashes kept getting worse. They kept getting more frequent. It got to the point where Marián was having to change his sheets every day because his skin irritation would cause some weeping, so he would go to bed at night and then his sheets would be soaked by the morning. He had areas of his skin which would stick to his suit. He'd have weeping onto his clothes. His shirt underneath his suit would stick to his body, and then he'd have to pull it apart.

What he ended up being diagnosed with was an irritant-induced eczema and we were constantly trying to find that irritant so we could eliminate it. We changed everything in a piece-by-piece way. We tried multiple different detergents, like the detergents that they use for newborn children. We tried changing his gear, so he never wore the same piece of undergarments twice. It was a constant attempt to try to find something that we could eliminate that would fix his given condition, but there just wasn't anything that was findable. We did allergy testing on Marián multiple times, and we never found an allergen. We never found any infection.

We think the heat and friction and sweat that happens when he had his equipment on was the culprit. Because he would come in after the summer, and the skin would be perfect because he just wasn't in the gear. He'd come in and he'd be perfect, but by the end of training camp, his skin would have blown up.

Eventually he was on steroids, often oral steroids. He'd seen a number of different dermatologists. Our dermatologist that looks after the team with us is fantastic, but he had seen other people, too, and nobody really had anything that would cure the problem. Everybody had things that would treat it. For a time, Marián was on a medication that we give people who have organ transplants so that they don't reject the organs that are transplanted. Heavy immuno-logic medications have risks, and it still wasn't fixing the problem. He was taking really heavy medication, so we're having to monitor his organ function because some of the medicines that he was on, those anti-rejection medications, are a big deal. So he's having to undergo blood testing constantly. We had to bring extra clothes on the road because he'd soak his shirt on the plane.

Just like anything with Marián, he was a warrior. He was fighting it, but it wasn't tenable. It just couldn't go on. We tried to do every-thing we could to manage it, but there was never any solution to fix it. And eventually, it got unmanageable, and that's what eventually forced his retirement.

When we announced that he retired, there were other teams that cried foul because of some contract stuff. So one of the things that we did at that point was to send him to a dermatologist that wasn't in Chicago, that was on the second medical opinion list for the league. And the note back from this guy basically said, I can't believe he's lasted this long. We didn't need to do that for Marián's state of mind. We needed to do it for the league. And I think it says everything about it. He tried everything he could. We tried countless things and it just wasn't tenable.

Thirteen

I wouldn't have had the career I did without the support I had at home from my wife, Jana, and my two daughters, Mia and Zoja. I've always thought it's important to have a positive home environment. If you don't, that's going to transfer over to the ice and your attitude in the locker room, whether you want it to or not. I strongly believe everything originates at home.

What you have at home with your family is so important in allowing you to go to work with a smile and bring the best possible you to your team. Jana provided that for me. She took care of everything. She allowed me to keep a positive mindset and to focus on hockey. When I went to the rink, everything was about hockey. When I came back home, I tried to leave everything back at the rink, but, honestly, most of the time I was still thinking about hockey.

Jana knows me better than anyone. She's been with me through everything. I wanted you as the reader to understand our partnership and family through her eyes and thoughts. She can help you understand me better too. Please meet my wife, Jana.

Jana Hossa

When I first met Marián, we were at a party. He asked me if I wanted to have a drink, and I told him I already had my drink. He got my number and asked me out for coffee a few days later. We've had coffee together every day since.

I knew he was a hockey player, but that's about it. I knew the Hossa name because his father was a national coach of Slovakia. My dad was a big hockey fan, and we'd always watch the World Championships together, so I knew Marián's dad but not specifically Marián, because I wasn't following the NHL.

My parents were worried when I first started dating Marián. I was just starting my studies at the university. They were afraid I'd quit school and go off with him. I was 19 years old, and I just fell in love. I didn't think about the future at that moment, but still wanted to continue studying. We were dating and just wanted to be together. What I liked about him in the beginning was he was a little older than me. He wasn't a crazy 18-year-old high school boy. I thought he was so normal, and I could talk to him about so many things. It worked between us. We became best friends.

We began dating during the NHL lockout. I didn't think then what our relationship would be like the next year or in the future. But that next season, he had to go to Atlanta, and we talked about me going with him. When you're 20, you just want to be with the person you love, so I didn't think too much about what it was going to be like. I was happy I was going with him and that we were going to be together in the United States.

When we got there, it was nice. We spent a few days together. But then he had to leave, and it started to become harder and harder because of the language, the culture and everything. I didn't know anyone. Everything was so big, so new, so different. We didn't have FaceTime, social media, or anything like that, so I felt homesick. It was also tough for my parents. Atlanta was much different than, say, Chicago. Chicago feels more European, more multicultural. I remember the accents were so difficult for me to understand in Atlanta. I thought because I had 10 years of studying English that I'd be fine, but I wasn't.

I traveled a lot back and forth from the U.S. to Slovakia for school. I did that when Marián was in Atlanta, Pittsburgh, and Detroit. I was in my last year of school when he was in Detroit, so I was traveling a lot that year. I didn't mind the travel because we got to be together, but it became difficult to get across the borders. I'd be questioned about why I was traveling so much. They didn't believe me when I told them why. I'd be detained for hours trying to get through customs.

I finished my degree in May or June of that year. All my friends were talking about their careers and their futures. I felt like I wanted that too. I had spent all this time studying, and I didn't want to just sit at home. At that time, I felt confused. I wasn't sure if I could continue living by his life as a hockey player and not working on my own career. That made for some more tough times. It wasn't that we didn't want to be together, but I had to deal with a lot of that myself. I had to decide if I could put my dreams aside.

Later, when I moved to Chicago and the kids were little older, I began planning my future more. I wanted to have things to do while they were at school. I was like, what are my possibilities? What can I do when Marián is at practice? I started taking yoga classes in Chicago and began planning little by little. It's different when you're in your 30s, a mother, and taking on something completely new. It wasn't like when I was a student before. But it became a passion for me. When we moved back to Slovakia, I started teaching classes at different places and began building my own business. But back when he was playing, I knew I had to support his career. I understood that early on. I saw how strict he was with training and hockey. He was always prepared 100 percent. He's just that type of person. He's very responsible, whether it's hockey or just him as a person. I understood that hockey was serious and important to him. I also saw how he grew up in a hockey family with his father, mother, and brother, and how hockey was always No. 1.

When he lost in the Stanley Cup Final two years in a row, it was difficult to watch, difficult to watch him. I saw how hard he took it. I could tell he was sad, but he always tried not to bring that home. I also didn't want to push him about it. I wasn't sure if I should ask about it or stop asking. Instead, I'd talk about our family stuff or whatever. If he needed to talk, we'd talk about it.

After he finally won the Stanley Cup, it was just beautiful. He was trying to achieve something for so long and he finally did.

The Slovakian flag made an appearance during the celebration parade in 2010

After the game in Philadelphia, they let the family members on the ice and I went to congratulate him. I could tell he felt so relieved. I remember we went to the locker room and it was just crazy. The celebration was awesome. I couldn't even imagine what Chicago was going to be like as a city after waiting so long to win the Stanley Cup. I remember the bus ride in the parade, it was like 2 million people or something. When I saw someone waving a Slovakia flag, that was just so nice.

We got married in Slovakia that summer. We had gotten engaged a few years earlier in Atlanta. It was nothing super romantic or anything. He proposed after his last hockey game of the season and he had reached 100 points, so it was a milestone for him, but definitely not a romantic proposal for me. We waited until I finished university to get married.

A few years later, we had our first daughter, Mia. There were a lot of mixed emotions for Marián at that time, because she was born two days after his friend Pavol Demitra had died in a plane crash. I remember after the crash we were watching the news the whole day waiting to get more information because we heard that maybe someone had survived. As we were watching the news, I started to feel a contraction.

It wasn't an easy day in the hospital. I was going through labor and he was sitting in the corner in his black T-shirt with his head down. It was tough because I needed support, but I knew he wasn't able to because of everything he was feeling. It was difficult. We were happy because she was born, but, on the other side, everyone was crying.

A day or two after I came home from the hospital, he went to the funeral. I couldn't go because I wasn't feeling good. I remember watching the service on the TV from the couch, sitting there with my daughter with tears in my eyes. And then in a few days, he had to leave for Chicago because the season was starting. I was stuck in Slovakia for a few weeks, and he was stuck over there. Marián doesn't cry, but he does get emotional. I know his face and can tell what he's feeling even if there aren't tears falling from his eyes.

At Northwestern Hospital in Chicago two years later, our second daughter, Zoja, was born. We literally lived right across the street from the hospital. I could see my apartment from my hospital room. Chicago will always be a special place for our family. Not just because of Marián's hockey success, but it's also Zoja's birthplace. Even after being gone for five years, the kids still often talk about Chicago and the places they remember. We love to look at the old pictures from those years in that beautiful city. We look forward to returning to Chicago with the kids and showing them everywhere we used to go when they were little.

We thought we were going to spend more years in Chicago, but our time was cut short due to Marián's skin condition. It was so difficult for me to watch him eat those pills to counter his condition. I just couldn't handle it myself anymore. I was so afraid of what would happen because of those pills. I wanted us to live more healthy and clean. I'm not a big fan of medicine and pills anyways. I try to find different ways to stay healthy if possible. I didn't want to see him suffer because of this.

His condition got worse over the years. That last season was definitely the worst. He was not OK. I saw it. He was nervous when the kids wanted to play with him and touch him and he was trying to be careful. Especially at night, he'd wake up and start scratching himself. Maybe if we had seen there were some new possibilities to treat it that he could have kept playing. Maybe that would have been different. But we didn't. We didn't have time to go through some long process. Sometimes those treatments take a long time. It's not like he was 25 anymore. I was so relieved when he stopped taking the pills. I remember exactly when he stopped. He took all the pills away and put them in the garbage, and I was like, OK.

After that, it's like we started a new chapter of our lives. He had to quit his job. We moved back to Slovakia into a new house. The kids started school. I started my job. It's like a chapter after hockey. The last year in Chicago we traveled to different places. We went to places I haven't been to in 15 years. We went to Hawaii, California. We took the kids to Disneyland and the Grand Canyon. We went to some places I've always wanted to go and show our kids while we were in the U.S. I really enjoyed it. It was great to be able to travel that year. It was never like that before because every year was up to his hockey schedule. That was everything. We didn't have weekdays or weekends.

With Jana and the girls at the Grand Canyon and the Hawks practice facility

Marián has always been great about having two daughters. He's never been like, I'm a hockey player and I want a son and for him to play hockey. He's always been happy with the girls. Right now, it may feel like they need their mother more than their father, but he has a great relationship with them. He takes care of them a lot these days,

On our first trip to Paris, in 2004

with me running my yoga studio. We've switched roles. He drives them to school and their activities. So, he's doing his job.

He's crazy about his technology. When he likes something, he likes it and he's not going to like anything else. Just like he was strict in his career, he's that same way with the things he likes. There are no discussions. He's always known everything about computers, iPhones, whatever is new. He knows all the details. Even the girls are always laughing about him and his phone. I always joke with him that if he wasn't a hockey player, he'd be a salesman for Apple.

Marián and I have been together for 20 years. I believe I've been a big part of his life and part of the puzzle for why he was successful for so long. I tried to provide him support and everything. He's a very normal guy and down to earth. He's very responsible as a husband and father. He's also very strict and responsible when he's focused on something, like his job. He knows what he's capable of. With Marián and me, it's always felt like he's my best friend and I'm his best friend. We talk about everything together. We live everything together.

Fourteen

In the big picture, Slovakia is a small country, but I'm proud to be from there and to have represented it as I did throughout my hockey career. There are only three players from Slovakia who were selected to the Hockey Hall of Fame. There's Stan Mikita, Peter Šťastný, and me. That means so much to me. We have our issues like anywhere else, including political ones, but it's where I grew up and it'll always be my homeland.

When I was born in 1979, there was one country, Czechoslovakia, and I was born in a small town named Stará Ľubovňa in east Slovakia. My mom, Mária, was from a small village called Podolínec that was nearby. We moved to Trenčín when I was two years old. My father, František, was at the age where he had to join the army. When he joined the army hockey team, he could have either played in Trenčín or with another team in the Czech Republic. Both teams were called Dukla. There was Dukla Trenčín and Dukla Jihlava. Bobby Holík, who I played with in Atlanta, was from Jihlava. My father went to Dukla Trenčín and had to serve two years in the army. After those two years, he decided he liked it there and signed another contract. So we stayed in Trenčín, and that's where I've lived most of my life.

Trenčín is a good-sized city with a beautiful castle in the heart of it. The city is known for its fashion and hockey. Since my dad was a professional hockey player, it was an easy choice for me and my brother to choose hockey. As little kids, my mom would take us to the stadium and we'd watch our

My parents and I, before I learned how to skate

dad play. That's how we fell in love with the sport. After the games, we'd go down to the dressing room. It was such a fun and special place for us.

My parents signed me up to play hockey when I was five yeas old. That's where it all started. First, we skated without sticks, which was not a whole lot of fun, but it was important to learn how to skate. Later, when our coach told us to bring our sticks to the next practice, it became much more enjoyable. Right away, I was trying to score goals. Even back then, I felt my hands were pretty friendly with the puck. Once we started practicing and playing with sticks, I couldn't wait for the next practice. It couldn't come soon enough.

Looking back, my brother and I got lucky in Trenčín, because we had great coaching from the beginning. My first coach when I was five was Coach Bakoš. From ages six to 10, our coaches were Pavol Opatovský and Jan Mikusik. When we were around 11, we went into the hockey program school. We switched schools and started attending the school next to the arena. Our coaches there were Pavol Sinkovic and again Jan Mikusik. Later on, we had Peter Bohunický and Pavol Bratranec as coaches, and then Juraj Boldiš. I played one year with the kids who were a year older than me, and we had Peter Matousek and Milan Cacho as coaches. When I was moved up to the men's A team, my coaches were Jaroslav Walter and Rudolf Potsch. I would never have become the player I did without the help of all those coaches. I'd like to thank them all for always teaching us, and especially me, something new. I know some of those coaches are no longer with us, but they were all part of my career and were great to play for. They were so important to me, which is why I had to thank them in my native language during my Hockey Hall of Fame speech.

When we moved to Trenčín, we lived in an apartment building that was provided by the army. Back then, it was still the communist times. The government built block after block of apartments. There was a playground beside each block for the kids to play sports. We had a playground right outside our window and grew up playing a variety of sports out there.

I honestly didn't realize we were living in a communist country. You don't pay too much attention to that as a kid. I only came to understand that as I got older. The communist government was brought down when I was 10 after people went to the streets and had a revolution. I remember there were big riots around that. We have some pictures of that time, but I don't remember a lot of it.

In 1993, Czechoslovakia split into the Czech Republic and Slovakia. When that happened, I don't remember much changing for me personally. It didn't affect me too much. My parents might have felt it differently. I remember my grandpa telling me the communist times were better because every-one had a job; there was no unemployment. That was true. But they also weren't paying people much and people weren't happy. Even if you had some great ideas, everyone had to make the same amount. But after communism was brought down and democracy came in, those smart people were able to start working on those ideas and make more money.

Because I was born during those communist times, my parents were limited in what they could name me. They wanted to name me Maros, but it wasn't in the Czechoslovakian cal-endar. So, the government told them they couldn't. They decided to name me Marián instead. You could only choose names in the Czechoslovakia calendar, because you had to celebrate the name days.

My family wasn't very political overall. My father some-times had to wear his military clothes, an army jacket and pins, but that was rare. Mostly, he was either playing or coaching hockey. My family was all about sports. To this day, I'm not very political. I understand it more now compared to when I was younger and my eyes are open to it, but that's about it. I certainly don't have any interest in being in politics.

One difference during the communist times compared to now is sports were paid for back then by the government. You could play hockey for free and everyone was allowed to play. Now it's much tougher. A lot of people can't afford to pay for the equipment, ice time, and travel while also providing for their family. Now it's mostly the upper class who can afford to put their children into hockey and other sports. After our generation and communism ended, we didn't produce as many NHL players as a country. You can see it in the NHL drafts. We didn't have as many players selected. We have some coming now, but it's not like it used to be. There was a lot of competition back then. If you didn't make a team, you'd have to go to a smaller city and play on their team and wait your turn. It made everyone better.

It was tough late in my career not having as many Slovakian players in the NHL. We couldn't assemble a team for the World Cup of Hockey in 2016. We definitely would have had a team in the past. There was me, Marcel, Zdeno Chára, Marián Gáborík, Pavol Demitra, Peter Bondra, Miroslav Šatan, Žigmund Pálffy, you name it. We had plenty of players, and good ones too. We were competing for medals in the Olympics and World Championships. It just wasn't the same when we had to put together Team Europe for the World Cup. People weren't as interested in Slovakia. On the other hand, if we did have a team, we would have struggled to compete as a country. We'd probably have given up a lot of goals. We have to accept that. We have to work with the young kids on the ice and improve our country's system to get more players to be at that level again. That's not easy to do, but I know there are people working on it. It is harder because there aren't as many parents who can afford to put their kids in hockey.

I remember some things about my dad playing as I watched him as kid. He was a big defenseman, 6-foot-2, 220 pounds. He was a stay-at-home defenseman. He wore the Gretzky helmet. Back then, everyone wore that, the old Jofa-brand helmet. My dad was a shot blocker. He had a heavy slap shot, but he was mainly a shot blocker. He didn't score many goals, though he did score one goal that was historic for our local team, Dukla Trenčín. We've tried to find it on video-tape, but we haven't been able to. When he was playing, the Czechoslovakia league would have the two worst teams play

My brother, Marcel, and our dad in the dressing room

for relegation; the winner would stay in the top division and the loser would go to the second division. Dukla Trenčín was facing relegation the one season with my father on the team. I don't think Dukla Trenčín had ever gone down to the second division. It would have been history.

In the relegation game, it was tied and went into a shootout. There wasn't any overtime. When the shootout began, my father was lined up as one of the last shooters to go because he wasn't much of a goal scorer. Nearly everyone went ahead of him. Old guys from that team joke that even one of the goalies went before him. During the shootout, every-one was trying to fake or make a move on the goal. When it was my dad's turn, he took the puck from the spot and began skating. Between the red and blue line, he wound up and took a slap shot. He surprised the goalie and scored. They stayed in the division, and it's considered a legendary goal in the club's history. I don't know what he was thinking, but he took a slapper from before the blue line. Like, who would do that? When he told me the story when I was a young kid, I thought he was joking. He got upset because I didn't believe him. I asked people who would have known, and they said it was true. No one could believe what he had done. It's too bad we don't have the video of it.

When I was in the NHL, I would also take slap shots during shootouts, but I was shooting them from really close to the goal and I was picking the corners. That was my move late in my career. I thought I could aim it high glove or under the blocker. I felt like I could beat any goalie with that shot. From the right angle, I felt like I had the advantage. The guys in Trenčín asked me if my style was the "old Frank" style. My brother and buddies would always joke about it. But I didn't do it because of my dad. I just felt like it was working. I would never shoot from as far as he did or with a wooden stick. I still can't believe it.

I came up through the Dukla Trenčín club myself. I played for their junior team and started getting noticed as a teenager. NHL scouts started coming to my games. During my draft year, I was brought up to the senior team. I had a really strong season. It was obviously a big jump going from junior hockey to men's hockey. It didn't take me long to realize I needed to get stronger. My shot wasn't that hard. I had to really work on that after practices. I knew I had some talent and quick hands, and my skating was pretty decent. I had to work on my strength and shooting ability.

We had a competitive and fun team. I was only 17 years old and the youngest guy on the team. I think everyone understood I had some ability. They weren't just putting me on the team because of my name or because Jaroslav Walter used to coach my father in the old days. Jaroslav left the organization, went to Germany to coach, and then returned.

He knew there was a young Hossa coming up and saw my potential. He gave me the opportunity to play. I have good memories with Jaroslav, who unfortunately isn't with us any longer. I wanted to prove I was worth that chance. There were a number of guys on that team that took me under their wing. We had some great older players. They were really friendly. When we did lose, they knew when to be a little bit harder on the younger players. But we really didn't lose much that season. They were nice to me. If I asked them something or needed a favor, they'd always do it. If I needed a ride, they'd drive me somewhere. They were a lot of fun and I had lots of laughs with them. We were winning, and it was an unbelievable atmosphere. I was still going to school and playing men's hockey. I was really enjoying myself.

My buddy Richard Lintner, whose nickname is Lemon, came up together with me on the team. He was drafted by the Coyotes a year before I was selected. As the youngest guys on the team, we were often responsible for cleaning the dressing room after practices. Once we had to clean our coach's moped bike. We had sprayed water on it everywhere, including where the cables were. He came out and told us we'd done a great job. We left and went to wait for our bus. All of a sudden, you could hear the coach struggling to start the moped. The bike had pedals, so he was pedaling it, but he couldn't get it going.

As he pedaled near the bus stop, we hid, so he wouldn't see us. To this day, Lemon and I laugh about that.

That season with Dukla's men's team, we won the championship. We beat Košice in the playoffs. You only had to win three games in those days. One funny thing I do remember is sitting in the locker room during the second intermission of the final game. A few players from the other team came over to the hallway by our dressing room. Then two of our top players, Ján Pardavý and Branislav Jánoš, went out to talk to them. As I understood it, Košice's players wanted to pay us to throw the game and allow the series to go back to their building. Our two leaders said there was no chance that we were going to do that. We were a really close group. We went on to win the game and became champions. I can't believe they tried to do that. I think enough time has passed to tell that story.

We won the Cup in 1997, and I became really close with my buddy Rasto Pavlikovský during that season. To this day, Rasty and Lemon are two of the closest friends I have. We played together on the national team for a few years. They were part of the Slovakia team that won the World Championship in 2002. Rasty attended training camp with me in Ottawa and Chicago. He and Lemon visited me in Chicago a number of times too. Rasty traveled to Chicago after we won the Stanley Cup in 2015, and we had a lot of fun together.

During that 1997 season, I also played for Slovakia in the under-18 tournament, the under-20 tournament, and in the World Championships. It was a unique situation where I was able to play in all three tournaments in one year. I especially played well in the U-20 World Juniors. I scored five goals in six games. I guess Marshall Johnston from the Ottawa Senators saw something in me to draft me 12th overall.

Aside from following in his path to Dukla Trenčín, my dad did influence me in hockey in other ways. He taught me discipline. I learned I had to sacrifice some things if I wanted to be good at hockey. Even if something else might seem more fun to do, I needed to dedicate myself to the game. That was tough at the time, and I didn't always understand him right away, but I realized later on what he was trying to show me. I had to stay home even if I wanted to go out with the guys. I couldn't be taking risks or drinking or whatever. I had to commit myself to hockey, go to practices, play in games, and dedicate myself to the sport. That's what I would do.

I remember when I was about 15 years old, Marcel and I were playing *NHL '94* or whatever Sega video game we were into then, and our father came home. He was surprised I was home and not at practice. I told him my hand was sore and I wasn't going to practice that day. He told us to turn the video game off and he took me to the rink. He said as long as you can skate, you can be on the ice. He was that type of guy. He thought I should be there regardless. That was a valuable lesson. At the time, I was almost crying and I couldn't hold the stick, but I skated just like he said. He wanted to teach me a lesson about determination and giving it 100 percent. He made his point. After that, whenever I tried to do something on the ice during my career, I knew I had to give it 100 percent or it didn't have meaning. That lesson was in my head. There are simply times where you can't play two games in a row at full steam, but I could always give it my full effort.

"I think Marián was like me, in that he was hardworking and disciplined," my dad told Scott. "When he was a kid and playing, I realized he wouldn't be going after me as a player because he was starting to score goals. I was more of a defender. Him and Marcel were scoring goals and making assists as forwards, and I was a defenseman, so they didn't take too much from me there. Players are more creative now and willing to go forward more than they did before. There weren't many offensive defensemen when I played."

My dad deserves the credit for steering my brother and me toward hockey. I was playing hockey and soccer, and at a certain point, you had to decide which direction you were going. Marcel and I decided on hockey because our dad was such an influence on us. We wanted to be hockey players, too, and it worked out. As for soccer, I was fast and could kick a ball, but I wasn't as skilled with my feet as I am with my hands. I'd kick the ball and run past everyone, but that was about it. So I think I picked the right sport.

I still love soccer to this day, though. I went with Marty Havlát and some buddies to watch the Euros in Portugal in 2004. It was fun to see how people really live the sport there and learn about the culture. Marián Gáborík, Pavol Demitra, Marcel, and I also went to the World Cup in Germany in 2006. It's special to watch those big games and they're a lot of fun. Gabby, Martin Škrtel—a former Premier League player—and I bought a suite in the new soccer stadium in Trenčín too. It's probably about 50/50 with people in Trenčín whether they're soccer or hockey fans. When there's a World Championship going on, everybody's a hockey fan, but during the Euros or something, everyone is a soccer fan.

My father stopped playing hockey when he was in his 30s and then he became a coach. While he was coaching, it'd be my mom who would drive us to hockey. She'd take us to practices and games because my dad was on the road quite a bit. I really have to thank her for that. My mom did a lot for us growing up. She deserves a lot of credit. I understand now how it's really on the parents whether their children stay active. They're the ones who find a way even if they're tired to get them to hockey practice or piano lessons. It was cheaper during communist times, but she was the one who was driving us or getting us on the bus. She was the one waking up every morning to get herself to her job at the clothes factory OZETA at 6 a.m. On the weekends, she'd get up early with us. That type of life isn't easy, but she was willing to sacrifice because she saw that we really loved to play hockey and that it made us happy.

My father came to our games when he could, but it was usually just my mother, Marcel, and me. We were used to that growing up. We would listen to my dad's games on the radio. There was one station that would give updates from stadium to stadium. My brother and I would be in front of the radio listening and my mom would be sewing in her room. Those are good memories. I definitely think I got my hands from my mother, because she was really quick with her hands.

I believe my dad is proud of Marcel and me for making it to the NHL. He knew it was our dream to play in the National Hockey League and for the national team when we were young. For me to be drafted 12th overall by the Senators and Marcel to go 16th to the Canadiens, as a parent, what else can you ask for? We were both first-rounders. I think they were both proud parents and enjoyed watching our careers develop.

"The first time Marcel and Marián played in Montreal, I was there," my mom told Scott. "Their father was coaching, so he couldn't be there. The TV [people] wanted to talk to me, and I barely knew any English. I'm not even sure what I said, but I said something. I was very emotional."

My mom remembered the first time I told her about Wayne Gretzky. He and Mario Lemieux were my idols growing up. Today, I have signed jerseys of both players in my home office.

"I remember when Marián went overseas for some tournament and brought home some trophy for top scorer or something," my mom said. "He brought home a card of Wayne Gretzky and told me he's the best player. I didn't know who Wayne Gretzky was. We were in a communist country and didn't follow these things. But Marián told me he's the best player and scored lots of goals. He was talking about Wayne Gretzky when he was eight. Later on, Marián got to play against Wayne Gretzky during his last game in Ottawa, in 1999. I was in the stands for that and remembered him bringing home that card. I was emotional. It was a beautiful time. I was just thinking how great that was."

I was hoping to get Gretzky's stick after that last game in Canada. But I was one of the youngest players on the team and there was a long line of players ahead of me who wanted the same thing. After the game, I shook Gretzky's hand, but I didn't get a stick. I do recall Igor Kravchuk got one stick from him, and I was looking at it like it was something magical.

I had a chance to play for my dad a few times in my career, with the national team. It was definitely special to play with my brother and to be coached by our father. My father was the head coach for the 2006 Olympics and was an assistant in 2010 in Vancouver. I imagine that was even more special for my mom, seeing her two kids and husband on one team. That was definitely a proud moment.

I was the team captain in the World Championships in Riga, Latvia, the year my dad was the head coach. He called me after we lost a game, and I remember we talked not as father and son but as coach and captain. That was interesting and different, and I enjoyed it. There were some good memories and some bad. We never got the chance to win a medal together. We finished fourth a few times and just missed out. That happened at the Olympics and World Championships while he was coaching. That's the one thing I wish would have happened. I was happy for him and my brother when they won a medal at the World Championship, even though I wasn't playing. I might not have a medal, but my family does, and I can live with that.

Playing in the Olympics was a dream come true. We had some great teams and I enjoyed being there. It was something special being in the village with all the Olympians and meeting interesting people from different countries and different sports.

In the 2006 Olympics, we were beating everybody, including Russia and Sweden, in the group stage, and we went up against the Czech Republic in the quarterfinals. We just had a block whenever we played the Czechs. We lost to them in the Olympics and the World Championship.

The Olympics in 2010 were great because Vancouver is a hockey city. It was great even just watching the games when we weren't playing. It was an unbelievable experience. We reached the semifinals that year and lost to Canada by a goal. I think we surprised a lot of people in that tournament. And then we played Finland in the third-place game. I think that was one of the most devastating losses of my career. We were up 3–1 after the second period and we were that close to making history for our country and winning a medal. But then we got into penalty trouble in the third period and lost the game.

I remember players were crying in the dressing room because we had come so close to doing something so special for our small country. It was a long walk to the dressing room. I got there, threw everything on the floor, and put a towel on head. I was starting to question whether I was going to win anything at some point. I hadn't won a Stanley Cup yet. I didn't know that was going to happen later in the year. I just couldn't believe it. I was like, really? I was getting so close, but I could never find that glory for some reason. It was first the 2008 Stanley Cup Final, then the 2009 Final, and now the Olympics. I was like, man, just give me a break. That was another thing for me to overcome.

ASIDE FROM THE national team, the other time Marcel and I played together was in Sweden during the 2004 NHL lockout. I joined the team Mora IK. There were a few NHL

Playing for Mora IK during the NHL lockout

players playing there already, including Daniel Cleary, Shawn Horcoff, Andreas Lilja, Ladislav Nagy, and my great friend Rasty Pavlikovský.

But as special as that experience was, more importantly, I met my wife, Jana, during that lockout. I say everything happens for a reason. We lost that NHL season, but I met my wife.

During the 2004 summer, before the season started, my friends and I would go out almost every weekend. One of those nights, I was out at a club. It was toward the end of the night, and I asked this pretty girl if she wanted to have a drink with me. She looked at me and was like, no, thank you. I told myself that was not an option, and I bought drinks for her and her friends anyway. I was later able to get her number from my brother. I texted her the next day and wrote that I had a few drinks the night before, and maybe we could grab a cup of coffee or tea instead. She was like, maybe.

A few days later, we had a cup of tea somewhere and started talking. At first, she had caught my eye because of her looks, but then I got to know her and really liked her personality. She was low key, easygoing, family oriented. That's what really got me going, her personality. And then we started meeting another day and another day and then I think she started liking me for me. Before that, I was Marián Hossa, the hockey player, but then she started liking my personality. That's how we ended up together.

When I went to play with Marcel in Sweden that season, Jana came for a few weeks. It was a big decision. She was already doing her first year at the university and her parents didn't want her to leave. We were trying to figure out whether we could do this long distance. The school later gave her the option to study on her own and return for the exams, so she was flying back and forth all the time. Then she went with me to Atlanta for the NHL season. Those first 2½ years were definitely a culture shock, but now we look back on that time fondly.

It's great being a dad of two girls, Mia and Zoja. Funny story about Mia being born: we knew our first child was going to be a girl and had started picking names. I remember going to the hospital, and I was sure the doctor had it under control, but I was panicking. The nurse came up to me and asked about the baby's name, so they could write it down. I'm like, Mia.

Then she asked, "What if it's a boy?"

I'm like, what do you mean if it's a boy? It's a girl, right?

The nurse said, "Yes, but there's always a chance it's a boy."

I had to make this huge decision by myself. I was thinking, my wife is going to kill me. I was really stressed for a minute. The nurse put so much pressure on me. I was about to have my first child and she's asking me to give her a boy's name, just in case. I told her, Mario. I don't know why I said Mario. I didn't say Marián, because I didn't like my name for a baby. But Mario was the closest alternative, and obviously Mario Lemieux was one of my heroes. I told my wife later what had happened and she started laughing. So we almost had a Mario. I know we could have changed the name, but it's funny because that nurse really caught me off guard.

I really enjoy being a girl dad. If I had boys, we'd probably be playing hockey. Not many girls play hockey in Slovakia; it's much bigger in the States. My daughters have figure skated and they've enjoyed it, but it's for fun and I'm not pushing them at all. I've been playing soccer with Mia. Our daughters are into their dolls and playing piano, and my wife takes them to gymnastics class. Boys are probably more trouble than girls. But as long as they're healthy, that's all that matters. I love my two daughters.

And, actually, I'm going to love having three daughters. As I was writing this book, Jana and I learned she was due with our third child, and, yes, we're having another girl. She should be here by the time you are reading this. Jana always wanted to have a bigger family and talked about having three kids. We had the first two and then waited awhile for the third. I'm excited for another girl.

The way I found out about the third is another funny story. We had gone to the Alps to ski around New Year's. Jana told me she wasn't going to ski one day. I didn't know it, but she instead went to the pharmacy to buy a pregnancy test. She had an idea that she might be pregnant. After the kids and I were done skiing, we went to the pool. I was there with them when I received a message from Jana with the picture of the test. I was like, what is this? Is this a COVID test? She doesn't feel good? But then I realized it wasn't a COVID test, it was a pregnancy test, and there were two solid lines. I'm like, huh. I replied to her that I would be up shortly. She was obviously expecting me to run to her immediately and give her a hug or something, but I was watching the kids in the pool and making sure they were OK. I was just really shocked too. It wasn't until the doctor confirmed it when we returned that I really believed it. I wasn't sure at first how to react when we discovered it was a girl again, but now I'm happy and the girls can't wait to have a little sister.

Late in my career, my oldest daughter was starting to realize I wasn't home as much and began to ask questions. She was still pretty young. But I knew if I kept playing, there would be more questions about when I was coming back. I know a lot of the older players have to go through that. I would obviously still love to play if it hadn't been for my skin condition, but retiring has also allowed me to spend more time at home. We traveled a lot when I stopped playing. It was nice to travel with the family instead of the team after so many years.

Overall, I try to be a good father. I think my parents did a great job with us. John McDonough would always tell me, "Marián, your parents did such a great job in how they raised you." They taught us how to be polite and gave us priorities in life. I want my kids to have a certain level of respect for people and I think it's always important to be grateful. I want them to be good people. We're hopefully setting good examples for them. Obviously everyone makes mistakes, but in the end, if you're a good person, you can be happy with yourself. My line has always been, treat people how you want to be treated. Not everyone's going to like you and you can't change everyone's mind, you have to be yourself. That's what I tried to do throughout my career even when things weren't great. In the hockey business, you're often under pressure, especially if you sign a big contract and there are expectations of you. I always tried to answer the media's questions and be respectful. I always tried to be the same person regardless of what was going on.

My daughters definitely remember going to the United Center. They spent a lot of time in the family room there. They'd go there between periods. When we returned to Slovakia, I think Mia understood more about me being a hockey player in America. There would be people asking me for autographs and pictures.

There was one time when we were on the playground. I was with my daughter and a friend of mine had his son there. I told my friend, my daughter's pretty skinny, but she's strong. She had been doing gymnastics. She showed them how she could climb the long handlebars at the end back and forth without problem and could just hang there. They were really surprised. My buddy then did the same thing, but he fell at the end. He then told me to do it and I told him, no.

My daughter's like, "Yeah, do it, Dad."

I'm like, are you sure you want me to?

She said, "Yes, it won't be a problem for you, you are Marián Hossa."

We started laughing. She was so cute. That was the first time I heard her say anything like that. I was blown away that she had formed that impression of me.

Our family has a dog now. I've had a few different dogs throughout my life. I once had a Weimaraner. They're called Grey Ghosts. It was like more of a hunting dog, but also a really beautiful dog. In Atlanta, Jana and I bought an English Bulldog. He was named Bono, like the singer; I'm a U2 fan. I think they're a great band. I saw them in Chicago at Soldier Field. That was a great experience. That dog was the coolest. It was easygoing. Now we have another dog, a Cavapoo. It's a poodle and a Charles Spaniel mix and her name is Gina. The dog was already named that, so we kept it. The kids picked the dog out. It's more of a kids' dog, a smaller dog. We got it from Hungary. Funny thing, she was born on the exact same day I was elected to the Hockey Hall of Fame: June 24, 2020. I guess Gina was just meant to be.

When I was a kid, we always wanted a dog, but we lived in a small apartment building. At the hockey stadium, there was a dog, a German Shepherd named Candy, and it would go on the ice with the Zamboni driver between periods. It was a big attraction. People loved it. At some point, Candy had some pups. My dad brought one of the puppies home when my mom was out of town. We were all happy...for two days. But my mom came home, and she's like, no way. She's like, this is going to be a big dog eventually and we have this small apartment. So we had to return it after two days. That was our childhood pet. She was right, though, it wasn't the smartest idea.

After my playing career, we started talking about where we wanted to live. I had spent 20 years in North America. I had favorite cities in the U.S. and Canada. We asked ourselves whether we wanted to stay in the U.S. or return to Slovakia. Jana wanted at first to come home to Slovakia, but then she wasn't so sure; maybe we'd stay in Chicago and raise the kids there. It was a small dilemma, but we knew in the end, everything would probably bring us back home to Slovakia. So we started building a house there. All of our family and friends are there, so there were a lot of reasons to come back and stay in Trenčín. Like I said, I'm very proud to be from here.

Fifteen

The 1992 Stanley Cup Final between the Chicago Blackhawks and Pittsburgh Penguins was must-watch TV for me and my younger brother, Marcel, even if the games were happening in the middle of the night for us. I was 13 and Marcel was 10. I don't even remember how we got each other up for the games at 4 a.m. or 5 a.m. our time, but we were awake for all of them. We shared a bedroom, awoke, closed our parents' door, turned on the TV in the living room, made sure the volume was low, and just watched the games unfold.

I remember watching the Chicago Bulls in the NBA Finals that year too. It's obviously rare for one city to have a basketball and hockey team in the finals in the same year, but that's what Chicago did. I enjoyed watching Michael Jordan. Who didn't? As I mentioned before, it was something to watch him in person later in life.

We all knew who Jaromír Jágr was, with him being from Czechoslovakia. He was playing at a high level then and really emerging as one of the NHL's top players. Plus, he was playing with Mario Lemieux, and I loved watching their two playing styles together. Mario had his magic going on. The Blackhawks were a good team too. They had Jeremy Roenick, Steve Larmer, Chris Chelios, and Ed Belfour in net. Mike Keenan was behind the bench for them. I remember they were taping a movie—*Sudden Death*—with Jean Claude Van Damme during the games at Pittsburgh's arena, and we later saw the movie just because of that.

Marcel and I would get up for the game and then remain up the rest of the day. We didn't go back to sleep and would head straight to school. I don't even know what we told our mom back then, but I didn't really care about the lack of sleep, because those games were so important to us. They were like watching cartoons for us. We had to see them and didn't care how we did so. We just wanted to see the best players play. I tried to study why Mario was so much better than everybody else. It was fascinating to watch players like that. I have a lot of great memories from that time. We were sitting there half asleep watching those elite players play hockey. The Penguins won the series in four games, but the games were competitive, and the Blackhawks could have won a couple of them.

Fifteen

Later on, Marcel and I both had a chance to meet some of those players during our own playing careers. They were the reasons we wanted to become hockey players and it was something special to meet them. I'll never forget shaking Mario Lemieux's hand and thinking about all he did for hockey and the city of Pittsburgh, and there I was standing across from him and having a conversation. It was the same thing with Wayne Gretzky. He came into Team Europe's locker room during the World Cup in Toronto in 2016 and I had a chance to talk to him. That's something I'll never forget either.

For Marcel, he got to play with Jagr after being traded to the New York Rangers in 2005. We had read Jagr's book as kids, which talked about his training methods after he had won two Stanley Cups. It was basically the first book we had ever read. He talked about his methods, including doing all his squats. Immediately, Marcel and I started doing squats. We were trying to do 500 a day, just like him. It was so inspiring for us. It's funny, but I went back to doing those 500 squats when I played for the Penguins.

Marcel remembered that too.

"In our small bedroom, we were doing squats," my brother told Scott. "We were paying close attention to Jagr. We were trying to be exactly like him. We were playing with the same exact hockey stick he played with. We both idolized him…. I got to play with Jagr, too, in New York. Sometimes we had phone calls when I was playing with him and Marián was asking about Jagr and all this stuff, and I was telling him stories. It was a fun time.

"I told Jagr about us reading his book. He was blushing. He's the type of guy who can take a joke and likes to make fun of himself. He's got a really good sense of humor. I can't believe he's still playing. He just loves hockey. I was privileged to play with these type of players. These are the stories I can tell my kids someday."

Marcel and I were actually on our good friend Richard Lintner's TV show not too long ago and he had taped Jagr for the show. We didn't know about it in advance. Jagr came on said, "Hey, Hossa brothers." He called Marcel his Czech brother, because he had liked playing with him in New York. He said, "Marián, big respect to your career and congratulations on the Hall of Fame." He said a lot of nice things. Jagr also said he heard the Hossa brothers were into boxing now and wondered if we wanted to get in the ring with him, then he showed his biceps. He finally asked us a question: "There's only one team I never lost to in my 30-year career. Can you guys guess which team it is? To help you guys, you can look at your passports." He obviously had never lost to Slovakia. We were laughing so hard. He's a pretty funny guy. I said on the show just how much of an influence he had on our careers.

Marcel and I have always been really close. There's almost three years between us. We've been playing hockey most of our lives too. I started skating at the age of five and my parents would bring Marcel, too, so he started skating even younger than I did. I always thought that's why his skating was a little bit smoother than mine. I skated funny when I was young. Later on, we started skating more similarly. That's also why people couldn't tell the difference between us when we had our helmets on. We were constantly playing hockey one way or another growing up. We played ball hockey outside and played hockey on the PlayStation inside. We'd also train together. We spent so much time together. We didn't have much of a sibling rivalry, though. We'd get into it sometimes, but probably not like most brothers. Marcel is pretty mellow and friendly. We never had too many arguments.

After I left Trenčín to play for Portland, Marcel and my mom came to visit me. He had a break from school, and I invited them to come over. Marcel was already bigger than me. The Winterhawks management got a chance to see him and his size. Július Šupler, who I mentioned before was from Slovakia and was a coach in Portland, mentioned to the Winterhawks ownership that there was another Hossa and he was probably going to be drafted high too. Long story short, Portland drafted Marcel and he played three years there.

Marcel was later drafted into the NHL as well, but I joke that I was drafted twice: the first time by Ottawa and then later by Montreal. I was sitting a few seats from Marcel at the 2000 NHL draft when Canadiens scout Pierre Dorion announced their draft pick. He said, "The Montreal Canadiens are proud to select from the Portland Winterhawks, Marián…uh, Marcel Hossa." Marcel didn't seem too bothered by it. I had to laugh about it.

If I had to describe Marcel, I'd say he's like a friendly teddy bear. He's a bigger guy, but he's really friendly. I always thought if he was meaner it might have helped him at times in his career. He's one of those people who never gets too worked up about anything. He's very chill. When something does really get to him, he's like a volcano. But it takes a lot for him to get mad and blow up.

Of course, people did start comparing us more and more as we got older. I don't think Marcel paid too much attention to it, but it's going to affect you in some way whether you want it to or not. There were probably times where if he had a different name he would have been looked at in a different way. If I had a brother who was older and people constantly compared me to him, that wouldn't be easy for me. When the reporters come in and start making those comparisons, you feel it. We never talked about it too much, but you definitely sense those things. He had it tougher and had to have a chip on his shoulder to play with the Hossa name.

Marcel did always handle it well, and that impressed me.

"It's a pretty psychological question," Marcel said Scott asked how he handled it. "You know, simple, I was OK with that. I don't know how to explain it. If someone is better than me, I can agree with this, even if he is my brother. There are some other guys who are better than my brother, and he's OK with that. For me, it was simple, and I agree to that, but my goal was to always get closer to him and achieve something like him. So, I can be happy."

Marcel had a great career. He played in 250-plus NHL games. He was the KHL scoring champion for a season. He played on the national team. He played in the Olympics. I've told him this a lot. There are so many players who would want to trade their careers for his. He had a lot of success. Not many players achieve what he achieved.

One of the shared passions Marcel and I have is for Formula One racing. We have both really gotten into it over the years. I've been to a few of the races. There was one year where Kimi Räikkönen, who was a Finnish driver, was skating with us in an exhibition game in Slovakia. I think we were doing some promo with McLaren Mercedes and Slovak hockey. Kimi was on a line with Marián Gáborík and me. I have a picture of the three of us on the bench The next day we were driving small motorcars in Bratislava. Later on, we were invited by the Mercedes team to watch a race in Hungary. Gabby, Marcel, and I went. We got to see behind the scenes—the pitstops, the paddock, everything. It was fascinating to see everything up close and study how they prepared for a race. We attended the qualifications and then the race. It was an amazing weekend.

More recently, we went to a race in Monaco in May of 2016. It was Gabby, Marcel, another friend, and me. We took a private jet there. We were invited that time by Red Bull

My brother and me in Monaco to watch a Formula One race

Racing. That was incredible too. I had never been to Monaco and that's one of the must-see Formula One races. We were set up with great seats as well and were given the VIP treatment. That was another special weekend.

There's something about Formula One racing that fascinates me. They're driving at such high speeds and have to be so focused. They're racing at 300 kilometers an hour and have so little room for error. They make one wrong move, and they could put their lives in danger. Like a lot of people, I also got into the documentary series on Netflix. It's drawn so many more fans to the sport. It's just so exciting. I really get into the races when I'm watching at home. We often watch them together as a family at my parents' home. I'm a big fan of Max Verstappen, who races for Red Bull Racing. One time I purchased Red Bull Racing jerseys for everyone, but Marcel didn't know about it. He showed up to our parents' house and everyone, my dad, mom, wife, kids, we were all wearing these jerseys. It was priceless. My mom recorded it. He walked in and saw the kids wearing the jerseys and didn't know what to say. He's like, what the hell is going on here.

As we've gotten older, Marcel and I have gotten even closer. Now that I'm back in Trenčín for good, we call, text, or see each other almost every day. I can actually see where he lives from my house. He lives right by my sport center. It's convenient for him because he's picked up golfing now too. We also hang out with the same people and go to the same places. It's special to me to have such a great relationship with my brother.

I didn't want to put any pressure on Marcel to say nice things about his older brother, so I was happy to suggest he and Scott talk on their own.

Marcel Hossa

I think every younger brother is looking to an older brother to set an example. When I was young, maybe I was 14, he moved up to play for the senior team in our hometown. From then on, I started looking at him more and more and was pretty much trying to do everything the same as him, especially on the ice. He was like a big mentor. He wasn't a teacher, but he was like my hockey idol. Everything he had when we were kids, I wanted to do the same. I tried to learn from him whenever we were on the ice. He was more talented than me hockey-wise. I knew I could take something from him and leave it on the ice. Those were good lessons for me when we were living so closely together growing up.

Our childhood was great. It was me, Marián, and our mom and dad. It was all hockey. For our parents, they may have put school first, but it was hockey for us. We were competitive growing up, but it wasn't too intense. I would beat him in some sports. We played a lot of tennis, especially when we came home after our seasons. We played a lot of ball hockey. We'd often play with Marián Gáborík and Pavol Demitra. It was a lot of fun. Marián could handle losing. You could joke with him about it. But the next day, he would try to kill you in a different sport.

When we were younger, we dreamed of one day playing in the NHL. I didn't realize we were good enough to make it. I remember he went to a peewee tournament in Quebec and he made a really good impression. There was a really nice article about him afterward. From there, people started talking about how he was going to be a good hockey talent. He also played on the senior team in his first year with our hometown team. He made a good name for himself and punched his ticket to the draft.

I was dreaming to make it there one day, too, but my path to the NHL was different. I knew I was going to fight people comparing me and Marián together. I knew in my head I was going to have to deal with it. But I also knew I could push myself to get to my dream in a different way. My path really started when I left for the U.S. at 16. That changed everything.

I was really excited to visit Marián and stay with his billet family in Portland. I didn't even speak English and it was my first time on a plane. It was a huge moment. For a young kid that wants to make it somewhere, they need to take that first step. Even if it's difficult in your mind and you want to go somewhere to chase your dream, you have to go forward. That week I spent in Portland, I loved everything. The hockey life, outside hockey, everything was great. I was really excited. Marián told me to bring my hockey gear, so I was practicing with the team for a bit. I was so thankful for that opportunity. They won the Memorial Cup that season and then the draft was coming. My agent called and asked if I wanted to start my junior career in the U.S. I was like, yeah, sure, right away. Everything worked out well, of course. I'm thankful to Marián because everything clicked together in my hockey life starting with those three years in Portland.

I'll always remember him getting drafted to the NHL. As brothers, we hugged. We clapped for him and watched him walk to the stage. I had goosebumps, for sure. My mom had tears in her eyes. My dad was definitely proud. To see Marián get drafted in a huge arena in front of a lot of people, it was a great feeling, a great moment. At my draft, they started saying Marián's name and then they're like, I apologize, I'm sorry, Marcel. Well, I'm like, that's a good start, you know. At that time, I didn't realize it. I only heard it later and we started laughing about it. It was a great moment, just like when Marián was drafted in Pittsburgh. Montreal drafted me in Calgary. It was another proud moment for our parents. I was happy that Marián was there too. He was already a star for Ottawa and had lots of media attention. I knew right away we'd have to deal with the media in Canada, because he was playing for Ottawa and I was in Montreal. I was ready for it.

The first time we played against each other in the NHL, it was Montreal against Ottawa, of course. I can't remember if it was in Ottawa or Montreal. I remember there was a lot of media for that day we stepped on the ice together. There were a lot of questions. But it was like any other game for us. We didn't want to make it a big deal, playing against each other as brothers. We wanted to act like professionals. I was definitely motivated to play against him, though. I don't know how he was before we played each other, but I was motivated, for sure. I wanted to prove to people around me, my coach, my team, that I deserved to be in the NHL. It wasn't always easy. My times in the show were up and down.

My best times were in New York, where I had the chance and privilege to play with Jagr on a line. Marián and I played against each other in the playoffs, when I was with the Rangers and he was with the Thrashers. I remember my parents were there for that. We beat them 4–0 in the series. Afterward, he wished me good luck in the next series. I know he was pissed off, because they had a really good team back then. He was playing with Ilya Kovalchuk. Coming into the handshake line, I could tell as his brother from the look on his face that he wasn't happy. But like any brother, he wished me good luck on the next round. For my parents, there had to be some mixed feelings in that situation, for sure. You don't know how to handle it, but that's life. He has three Stanley Cups and is in the Hall of Fame.

It was a big moment for our family when I, my dad, and Marián were together on the national team. My dad was coaching. It was a huge deal for our mom. It was a fun time. It was a proud time for our mom and dad. I have pictures of us together in my home. Those were great memories and just a great feeling. I remember one game in the World Championship where I set Marián up for a goal, but we weren't often on the same line. The first time we played together on a team outside of the national team was in Sweden playing for Mora during the NHL lockout. He came over to play with me for a month. He had been playing in Trenčín with Gáborík and Demitra. He decided to try something different for a little bit and Dukla agreed to that. He played for two teams in one season. It was a fun time to be around him. It was like a junior league for him at that time. He was making plays and the arena was full because everyone wanted to see him. The young kids in Sweden wanted to see him. It was a great time.

When he won his third Stanley Cup, I came to Chicago to see the Blackhawks play Tampa Bay. I had been back home in my apartment and watching every game like a fan, staying up late. He called me after they advanced to the last series and asked if I wanted to come. I'm like, really? I decided two days before Game 6 to go. I thought it was a once-in-a-lifetime chance to see him win the Stanley Cup in person. I jumped on the plane, arrived at their apartment, and went to the game. I was really proud of him and happy I had gone. I went to all the celebrations and everything when they won the Cup. I tell all my friends, when you win the Cup, it's tough, but it's tougher when you're drinking and celebrating. You're not sleeping, just partying, that's tougher to heal from. I stayed about a week. It was really exciting to meet his friends and celebrate with the team. I was really privileged to be there and enjoyed that time with him. It was fun to be on the parade bus and go through the city and finish it at Soldier Field.

I never tried to think of it as me and my brother competing. We were raised to stay humble, and everything happened for a reason. We were chasing our dream. It wasn't my brother who built my way to the NHL. It was me who had to fight for a chance to stay on a team. Everyone is building a name for themselves when they step on the ice. I guess I had a long and healthy playing career. I had some ups and downs in the NHL and the farm team for 10 years and then eight years in the KHL and a couple years in Europe. It was a fun ride.

Marián and I respect each other. As we're getting older, we've become closer. We're not kids anymore. We have our own hobbies and things we like to do. But you know, he's my brother, I'm going to always be behind him no matter whether it's good or bad. I'm sure he'll do the same with me. When I look back at our times as kids, the time flies by so quick, and life goes on. It's a different chapter now for us after our hockey careers, but we're having fun with that too.

Sixteen

Here's everything you need to know about the difference between Marián Gáborík and Zdeno Chára. Before Gabby and I played in the Western Conference Final in 2014, he came over to my place in Chicago the night before and we hung out. Before Big Z and I played in the 2013 Stanley Cup Final, I didn't dare ask him to meet up. I knew how he would have responded.

Gabby and Big Z are totally different, but I get along with both of them. We all grew up in Trenčín. I knew both of them when they were really young. Gabby is a little younger than me and Big Z is a little older. Big Z's personality is really professional. It's why I didn't bother asking him to meet before the Cup Final. Gabby's a competitor on the ice, but he's more laid back. He's up for some company and just talking.

All three of us obviously have won the Stanley Cup. Coming from the same small Slovakian town which has fewer than 60,000 people, that's already something special, but you add in that we all now live on the same street and that's *really* special. The neighborhood we live in is called Pod Brezinou, and is located right under the woods near Trenčín Castle, which is named after Matúš Čák III Trenčiansky, who was a king who once lived there.

Growing up, we all lived in different neighborhoods of Trenčín. But as we started getting older and playing in the NHL, we all gravitated to the same street. There had just been woods in this area before and then they started building some nice apartments. My mom recommended I buy one after I started making some money in the league. Pavol Demitra also bought a place. Big Z and Gabby did too. You know how it is when one person buys something pretty lucrative and it's in a good neighborhood. Buying an apartment here made sense for all of us, as we were in North America for 10 months playing and then back home in Slovakia for two months. None of us needed a big home yet. But the neighborhood is near the castle and close to the city, and there's really no other area like this in Trenčín. So, we all ended up here and later won a total of five Stanley Cups between us. There was a story in the newspaper asking whether the name of the street should be changed to the Stanley Cup Street or something.

They asked us and we were fine with it, but we knew a lot of people would be against it. It would be a lot of paperwork and hassle to change it. I'm sure people would be annoyed with it. Still, it's really unique. I don't know of anywhere else in the world that has so many Stanley Cup winners on one street.

When we were growing up, we would come by these woods often. We'd run figure eights around the woods. All the different age groups would come there to train with their teams. I know these woods really well. When I take my kids to them, it reminds me of when I was really young and living on the other side of the woods. Back then, all the neighborhoods had apartment buildings that had been built during the communist times. We grew up 15 minutes from where I live now on the other side of the woods. I started on that side and now I'm on this side.

I bought that first apartment around 2000 and later bought property on the same street and have since built a house there. Gabby lives about a 30-second walk from me and Big Z lives about 30 seconds from him. I'm at the end of the street, Gabby's in the middle, and Big Z is a little farther down. Pavol Demitra's wife also lives on this street. There are also some other guys who played hockey outside of the NHL in our neighborhood. Martin Škrtel, a pro soccer player, also lives here. You could put together a pretty solid hockey lineup from our one street. You got six or seven guys who played professionally. We'd probably need a goalie; I don't think any goalies live here.

I FIRST MET Big Z before I had played in juniors. He was two years older than me. He was usually playing for the B squad when he was younger because he was so awkward with his skating. No one had the proper-sized equipment for him. The skates were too small. His stick was too short. He had pants that looked like shorts on him. You'd laugh at him back then. He was a skinny kid and just battling for his life. He didn't have any skill. He struggled to skate and had little mobility. It's amazing what he's done with hard work. He went to work out with his dad, who was a wrestler. He'd train with all these wrestlers and they'd throw him around like a bag of rice. But he gained strength and lost all his fear while doing that. He was smart back then and left Slovakia for a year, because he didn't feel like he was going to get a chance to play much here. He went to play in Prague and got drafted to the CHL. There, he got proper equipment, skates, and started looking like a real hockey player.

I played up with the older kids in juniors, so I would play with his team. During the summer, we'd go to the Liptovský Ján area to train for a few weeks with our team. We'd wake up and run in the morning and then have practices later in the day. We'd also play different sports for conditioning. I remember everyone wanted to be on Big Z's team when we played basketball because of his height. I was around 15 or 16 when we started getting closer. We've become better and better friends since then. Later on, we started playing together with the national team and then he was traded to the Ottawa Senators from the New York Islanders when we were both in the NHL. We were both later traded from the Senators to other teams, but we were pretty tight by then.

Having Big Z in Ottawa was great. You had a friend, teammate, and countryman, someone who was from your hometown. We had a lot of laughs during those years. He's obviously an animal with his training. He trained mostly by himself, but we'd join him here and there. We'd attempt to do what he did, but we just couldn't. He's still such a positive person. He was like, "OK, you don't have to finish it in time, just do it even after the time limit, just finish it." You'd have to do like 15 exercises in a certain amount of time. After you're done with that, you'd have to climb a rope. I just couldn't finish it. I was burning my hands on the rope. I told Big Z, "Forget this, I'm not doing this anymore." He was laughing. He's like, "Do it once and you don't have to do it again, and I'll do it three times." We just went to watch him. He was a maniac.

I did reach out to Big Z before the Blackhawks played the Boston Bruins in the 2013 Cup Final. After we both finished the conference finals, I called him. I knew once the Stanley

Cup Final began that there wouldn't be any communication between us. He'd be all business then. We had a good chat before the series, though. I told him I knew we probably wouldn't talk again for a few weeks and he wouldn't be speaking to me on the ice. We both knew we'd be friends afterward.

Back in 2013, Big Z was one of the top defensemen in the league; he had won the Norris Trophy in 2009. He played so many minutes. As a team, we spent a lot of time talking about how to play against him and how to beat him. I remember we discussed wanting to pass the puck through his big body on the power play, because there were holes he couldn't fill due to his size. He obviously had a lot of range, but we tried to use some of his weaknesses to our advantage. He was mobile for a big defenseman, but you could also exploit that. If you shift one way and then another or put the puck behind him, it would take him a lot of energy to make those type of turns. We knew he was going to play a lot, but we wanted to make those minutes tougher. We had a game plan to try to beat this giant defenseman. I was on the ice with him a lot in that series. As I mentioned before, he didn't care that I was his neighbor and friend. He had no problem cross-checking me as if I was anyone else.

We didn't talk during the series, as I expected. Luckily, I was on the winning side when the series was over. In the handshake line, we hugged and shook hands. He congratulated me, but there wasn't much to say. The first time I saw him after that, I didn't say anything either. I thought it was best not to bring it up. We've since talked about the series and especially Game 6. It was such a tough game and came down to the end. We were down a goal late, pulled the goalie, tied the game, and scored again to go ahead. We scored twice in 17 seconds. I think the Bruins were in shock. I told him, who knows what would have happened if we went back to Chicago for Game 7? We would have definitely had some pressure on us at home. Boston just couldn't score that one goal, and all of a sudden we scored two.

Big Z has continued to play in the NHL. Before the 2020–21 season, we had a long talk. He was turning 44. We had met when we were like 13 or 14. Other NHL players still have so much respect for him at the front of the net. He's such a great leader on and off the ice. He still works so hard. But what I told him was, I don't understand what he talks to 20-year-old players about. He's like their father. He's double their age. I would have wanted to finish my career just because there would be nobody else around my age. I told him, if a player slashes him on the ice, they probably say, I'm sorry. They have to show some respect for a 44-year-old. He laughed when I told him all this. He said some of the players just don't have any respect for their elders. He did say the referees do talk to him a little differently because they do have respect him.

Big Z is such a great story. This young, awkward-looking hockey player became this Norris Trophy winner and Stanley Cup champion and has now played the most NHL games by a defenseman in league history. I have a lot of respect for Zdeno Chára. There's no question he'll also be joining the Hockey Hall of Fame one day.

AS FOR GABBY, he and Marcel grew up and played together. Their games would be right after our games, so I'd be there to see them play. Gabby was always a goal scorer. You could see the speed, quickness, and wrist shot in him. Marcel played center and was always setting Gabby up. They were three years younger than me. I first started playing against Gabby in the NHL when he joined the league as an 18-year-old. We later started playing together with the national team and played for Dukla Trenčín, our local team, during the 2004–05 lockout season. He, Pavol Demitra, and I played together for Dukla that season. When the team really needed a goal, the coach would load up a line with the three of us together. We played a fast game. Gabby had so much speed and a laser shot, and Pavol would give us perfect pucks with his hockey IQ. We had a lot of fun together.

During the 2013–14 season, when we met in the conference final, he had been traded from the Columbus Blue

Jackets to the Los Angeles Kings at the deadline. The Kings made a run and reached the conference final. The first game was in Chicago. If it was the regular season, it wouldn't have been a big deal if we got together. But in the playoffs, there's sort of an unwritten rule about being too friendly. He was staying at the Ritz-Carlton, which was about 100 meters from where I lived. I was home alone, he had nothing to do, and we texted to meet up. We made sure to do it quietly. He came over, had dinner, and chatted. We just relaxed and talked. We watched some Slovak TV. I had some Slovak and Czech TV channels, so I could catch up on the news and sports back home. Unfortunately that series didn't end as well as the one against Big Z. We lost to the Kings and Gabby in seven games, and they went on to win the Stanley Cup.

Gabby and I have gotten closer as we've gotten older, and especially since we've both retired. We live the same lifestyle in the same city and are both on the same street. We have our own things going on, but we get together for coffee, sometimes have dinner with our wives, and watch the local hockey and soccer teams together. We pretty much like the same activities. We hang out with Marcel too. Gabby has a house in Croatia, and I recently bought one out there that is about 25 minutes from his.

Of our local players, Tomáš Kopecký, who lives right next to Trenčín, was the first of us to win the Stanley Cup.

He won it with the Red Wings in 2008 and another with the Blackhawks in 2010. When it was my turn, I thought the castle would be a great place to have a party. There had been other events up there before. You could envision how magical of a night it could be with the Cup and views of the city from the castle. That last year, we had Blackhawks flags on the castle. Once we had it there, it was tough for anyone to beat that location. Big Z and Gabby would later both have their Cup parties at the castle too.

Big Z won the Cup with the Bruins in 2011. He had a nice party in the castle. I had my second Cup party in 2013. When Gabby won it in 2014, he definitely took his Cup day to an even higher level. I do think my 2015 Cup party was a special one. We kind of knew what we wanted to do and who to invite to make it right. The first Cup party was more like people ripping off their shirts and throwing them down from the castle. It was more like old times in the Cleopatra club where we used to go. The 2010 party was a wild one. Come 2015, we were older and more mature. We got more dressed up, included the family and friends, and had great programs and entertainers. It was really cool in 2015.

My agent Peter Neveriš and Miro Kubis took care of the arrangements for the Cup parties. Big Pete especially has been there for me through everything. He lived next door to our apartment growing up and was there playing ball hockey with us every day. We became closer friends from that early age and he's like a second brother to me now. I know I can trust him with anything and that he's always there for me.

With that 2015 Cup party, we had an army band play. That was something really different and cool. We had a popular radio and TV duo, Junior and Marcel, come emcee the event, and they were great. I was able to have time with the Cup with my family, but also everyone could take pictures at the castle. We had a legendary pool party with it at my parents' house. We had a parade with the Cup through the town. There's a tradition of everyone eating something out of the Cup and I kept it up, so I went with my favorite potato and cheese pierogi.

With my good friends Zdeno Chára and Marián Gáborík at the 2012 NHL All-Star Skills Competition. It is so special that we all came from the same small town and now live on the same street. *(Getty Images)*

Especially in east Slovakia, that's the most popular pierogi. It's the kind we make in my company. It was an amazing two days with the Cup in 2015. I think I slept for two days after that because I was so tired. It ended up costing about 100,000 Euro, but thanks to great sponsors I don't think it cost me much in the end.

During those two days in 2015, we had the idea to get Gabby, Big Z, and me together with the Stanley Cup on our street. Peter Neveriš made the phone calls and got everyone together. Everyone put on the jersey of the team they won the Stanley Cup with. I wore my Blackhawks jersey, Gabby had on his Kings jersey, and Big Z had on his Bruins jersey. We stood beside the Stanley Cup on our street and took pictures. It was a great moment and will always be a great memory.

GABBY AND BIG Z were willing to share their thoughts on our friendships and careers with Scott.

Marián Gáborík

Marián is three years older than me and I kind of had all the same steps in his path, except the juniors and everything. He left earlier. We're from the same hometown and ended up pretty much living on the same street. We started in the NHL around the same time. We ended up signing in free agency around the same time. He signed the 12-year contract, and I signed five- and then seven-year contracts. And then we ended up retiring kind of at the same time.

During the 2004–05 lockout, we talked about where to play along with Pavol Demitra. They just wanted to stay here in Trenčín and play for Dukla. There was an exchange period where you could trade teams for a bit, and we decided to go to Sweden and come back. We talked about it and wanted to come back for the playoffs. So we went to Sweden. He played with Marcel and I played with Chára on Färjestad. I was there for a month. He was there maybe longer. We ended up coming back and finishing the season here. We had a tough loss in the quarterfinals against the capital city, but it was fun. Even though you want to play in the NHL, that was dragging along and you didn't know if the season was going to happen. That was different. I know he was getting offers from Russia and I did, too, but we wanted to play here and experience the atmosphere we got to know when we played for the pro team when we were 16, 17 years old.

The atmosphere is amazing. A lot players from Czech and Slovakia who got to play in the NHL played here, even Vladimír Růžička, Žigmund Pálffy, Miroslav Šatan, Róbert Petrovický, Róbert Švehla, all these guys were playing here. So growing up, I remember it was always a packed house. As kids, we were sitting on the stairs because there were no empty seats, so we kind of snuck in. The overall atmosphere in Europe, it's a little different from the NHL, but people really love their hockey here.

It's going to be 60 years for Dukla Trenčín in 2022. There's a lot of history here. Marián's father played here. He helped the team stay in the league with his famous slap shot penalty shot. He coached here too. We grew up through the system here, me, Marcel, and Marián. It's not like America. Here, every professional team has to have teams below, like junior teams, kids teams, so you grow up through the system, and we ended up fulfilling our dream by playing for the pro team. With new ownership now, they're going to do things differently. They want to do it the right way. You can see with the arena, they're trying to renovate things, build new things. The owner is a true diehard Trenčín fan, a philanthropist who's putting his heart into it.

Marián and I dated American girls, Canadian, and it was all good and fun times, but at the end of the day, it's a different culture there and we always wanted to settle here. I love the U.S. and everything. It's my second home, but this is where my heart is, my home, my family, my friends. I remember during the season when we were out in the U.S., toward the end of the season, we were always excited to come back here and get together, whether it was to go out, get together to play different exhibition games, soccer games. We have a big group of guys that are from here and stay here and train here during the offseason. We always wanted to come back here and live here. It's a nice little town with a lot of history. Some guys from this area decide to move to the capital city, Bratislava, but we have nice privacy and people know you. We were always wanting to come back and live here.

I still get goosebumps thinking of winning the Stanley Cup. It's pretty amazing. Especially for Marián, we talked a lot about the back-to-back finals he went to, and then exchanging teams and playing against your previous team. It must have been so hard for him. I can't imagine how he must have felt. I know he had offers from Edmonton for this crazy amount of money. Some people would say, this isn't meant to be, I'll just go for the money and settle for whatever team. But he was determined to still go after it. After that, he was down that summer and signed with Chicago, and the third time's the charm, I guess. I couldn't be happier for him. We watched all the games at Marcel's place with the guys. It was kind of a consistent routine where we watched it at his place.

So then, yeah, he won. Then Chára brought the Cup, then Marián again, then me, then him again. It started to get kind of normal. You know, who's gonna bring the Cup next? Three Stanley Cups and I was at all his parties at his parents' house and then the castle. We were running out of ideas what to do with it. The picture we took of all three of us was pretty special. One street, pretty much 100 meters from each other, and five Cups. If you count Tampa, six. I'm kidding. But it was pretty special, and to celebrate here and at the castle was a perfect place for it. We have respect for each other. We really cheer for each other. I think everybody could sense the genuine excitement and happiness we have for one another.

We played Marián and the Blackhawks in the 2014 conference final. Marián and I met in his apartment before the series. We didn't really talk a whole lot about hockey. It was just a regular meet-up and we caught up. I remember he had a beautiful place in Chicago. You see that people loved him there, and those guys who won three Cups were a huge part of it. After he couldn't play anymore, you could see the Blackhawks really missed him. He had become a two-way forward. He took pride in going forward and it was almost better to come back and steal the puck from somebody. My opinion is he got that from Datsyuk a little bit—not a little bit, a lot—when he played in Detroit. I remember him telling me they played a little game where they kept the puck away from each other. I think he started loving that and took it with him to Chicago and it was a huge part of his success.

I think I can speak for him about how his career ended. It would have been worse if your body couldn't play but your head wants to. It would be much harder from that perspective. But I think we were both on the same page in terms of the mind was accepting the body, and that way the departure was easier. Obviously, we like to follow the game and everything, but we're OK that we're not playing anymore because we can't.

Marián's enjoying his life now. He's got two beautiful daughters, has his business going on, and he's busy. He's not bored, which is great. You know how it is with a lot of retired guys, that after retirement they can go south, but he keeps himself in good shape doing his boxing. He seems very happy, so he's enjoying his retirement, for sure. You can see he's always in a good mood. He loves taking care of things around the house. He likes his gadgets. He always has everything like top notch, whether it's his robots mowing his lawn or whatever. Everything has to be clean. He has a bike. He has a little stand where he cleans the bike and all his products. He's like a little monk in terms of everything. Everything has to be in order and perfect. Marcel is worse. He probably washes his car three times a week. His closet has to be perfect. Really the details of everything have to be perfect with Marián. You can see it with his house, his gadgets from Apple, everything has to be brand new. Everything that comes up on the market, he has to have it. They're both like that.

Marián has made a name for himself and put this town and Slovakia's name out there as a place that produces great hockey players. He beat everybody from this country winning three Cups. He made a big statement for this community and for the whole country too. I'm proud of what he's done on the ice. And obviously he's a regular guy. He's not cocky. He's grateful and a down-to-earth guy. He's a great guy to be around.

Zdeno Chára

I knew Marián when we were kids. We didn't play together in the same class. He was a bit younger, but I do remember meeting him because obviously his dad was a big-name player in the old team Dukla Trenčín. Both of his sons, Marián and Marcel, were well known. I think that everybody kind of saw at a young age both of them were very talented.

Once I got traded to Ottawa, we got to know each other much better, and we got much closer, coming from the same town. At that time, Marián had his mom living with him. We had a number of Slovaks and Czech players on the team, so we were always hanging out together, spent a lot of time on the road together. It was kind of super unique, because I think at some point there were seven of us, and that's quite a big number. If you consider you have a 22-man roster and you have seven, so that's probably a third of the team, Czech and Slovak players? We had quite a few Swedish players, some Finn players, one or two Russians, so it was very much a European team. We had some success in Ottawa, winning the Presidents' Trophy one of those years and we had a pretty good run. We lost in the semis against New Jersey in Game 7.

We were from not just the same country, but the same town. We grew up playing for the same hockey team. That obviously made a lot of things, whatever we talked about, a lot of things were in common. Our parents knew each other. It was just really easy.

I think we created so many NHL players here because growing up and experiencing the atmosphere and watching the men's team playing and winning the championship, back then it was the Czechoslovakia championship, seeing what a great atmosphere it used to be at the rink and the games, we all kind of got motivated by it. I think that was pretty unique. Most of us attended a school that allowed all the players from each level to be in the same class. It wasn't a sports academy school, but I think that created kind of like a bond, and we had some advantages as far as being able to train and skate either before school started or sometimes during the school hours or after. So the program allowed us to spend a lot of time practicing and being together.

Marián is very easygoing. He's a guy who loves to have fun. He doesn't look for trouble or to get into conflicts or disagreements. He loves a relaxed atmosphere. Anytime we got together, he always wanted to have a fun, loose atmosphere where we kind of sit around and talk about stories and jokes and all that stuff. So he enjoys that.

Every time we were getting ready for the season, we would be skating for like a month, month and a half, and we'd all be grinding on the ice and working extremely hard to be in the top shape and feeling good and feeling the puck and basically feeling as comfortable as we could be going into training camp. And Marián would show up, probably the latest on the ice of all of us, and he'd still be the best. It was almost mind-blowing that he would step on the ice for the first time after the whole summer and basically dangle everybody and just score goals so easily.

To me, he's got incredible vision and feel for the game and was very explosive. He's a strong guy and I'm very impressed that he changed his game to be a very valuable two-way player. I think early on in his career he was very focused on producing offense and scoring goals. Huge credit to him that he realized that he could also help the team playing really good defense, by backchecking and getting some takeaways and blocking shots and being on the penalty kill. I think he really embraced that role and was one of the top two-way players in the league. I said many times that I was shocked that he was not even considered to be nominated for the Selke Trophy. I think most of the times those are the centermen because the faceoff stat plays a huge role in that category. I know he maybe didn't take many faceoffs, but he was as good as I've seen backcheck or play a 200-foot game, where he was going up and down and really helping the team on both ends of the ice. That was very impressive because I'm sure that wasn't easy for a player to probably sacrifice 20, 30 points a season to be more defensive. But he was willing to do that, and it rightfully paid off for him. He's got three Stanley Cups and I'm sure that played a huge role in why Chicago was able to win.

Most of the Slovak NHL players were forwards. I was in a different position as a defender. I ended up matching up and playing against most of the top players and lines. For me, I had to put myself in a position to disconnect from kind of the relationships or anything going on during the game, because I knew I would be competing against them. I had to be on top of my game and be sharp. Marián was one of those guys who understood that better than any others. Some guys didn't take it as well when I played them hard and I finished checks on them and I was physical against them. I think it would be very unfair if I played certain players easier or harder just because of the nationalities or friendships. I'm a professional, and once I put the jersey on, I play for the team. I wear the jersey and whether there's an American, Canadian, Slovak, Czech, Swedish, Finnish, I really don't care. I'm gonna play the same way against whoever is standing against me.

Marián understood that's my game, that was part of who I was as a player and I had to play a certain style, and so he was completely fine with that. He knew sometimes we'd go out for dinner before the game and we would have a great time, but the next day, I would play against him very hard and he understood that. So that was a good thing about him that he knew that. Hey, both of us had jobs to do and I was kind of on the side where I had to initiate, and he was the guy who tried to score goals and I was trying to defend him.

I think we called each other before the 2013 final started, and we said, hey, we'll be playing for the Cup and we will have to put everything on the line and may the best team win, and that was it. I think we both knew what was at stake. It would be unfair to our teammates or to our teams if we would not play to our 100 percent potential and give everything that we had for our team. He understood that and I understood that. That was clear. When it was that point of the season, you got to do what you got to do. I think we talked again after everything was said and done, in Slovakia. I mean, during the handshake, we exchanged a few words, but that was it. I knew he was busy with the celebrations and I was obviously moving on.

When he won the 2010 Cup, I was with the family watching the game and we were in Florida on a little break. I remember seeing him raise the Cup. I called him the next day and I was surprised he picked up. I think I sent him a text message and then called him the next day. He was extremely happy. He was so relieved that finally it happened for him after two losses in the finals, and I was extremely happy for him as well. Seeing him obviously succeed and being a Stanley Cup champion, that was actually very nice. I was happy for him.

The person organizing the Cup parties back home had to be very creative, so it didn't become kind of the same old thing. We had the Cup in the same city seven times. And it was pretty much the same person who was organizing the Stanley Cup parties for every player. He obviously had very good experience with managing everything and putting everything together. When you have the Cup year after year after year after year, it becomes like, OK, what am I gonna do now for this player? What am I gonna do for something new? Pretty much most of the friends we have back in a Trenčín we share, so it was one of those things where you want to throw it so it's not boring for the audience, it's not something that's just repeating. Even if it's very special for the player, you want to also entertain the families and the friends, and you want to share that Cup with the city and make it very nice. For most of us, it happened once, for Tomáš Kopecký twice, Marián three times, so obviously he had the upper hand because he was obviously able to be more creative with it

It's really nice that most of us have a championship. Nobody even imagined that all of us could be champions. It's great that Marián and Tomas are multiple-time champions. As we all know, it's luck sometimes. It's just the way it goes. But I think it's great that we were all able to come out of such a small town and be valuable pieces in the history of the clubs we played for and be able to share those memories of winning the Stanley Cup.

Once you get older, you have family and try to settle into places that are most comfortable for you and your family, so we ended up very close to each other on top of the hill in Trenčín. Marián and Gabby, they built big houses. I have a house, but it's not in Trenčín. It's a little bit in a mountain area. But I have a nice condominium there where I'm able to be comfortable with my family. But it's very unique that we live on the same street.

I wasn't surprised when Marián announced about his skin condition. We had talked about it probably two years prior, that he was experiencing some problems with his skin. I had a chance to see it firsthand at the World Cup. I saw that he was getting really bad. He said he was considering retirement because basically the medication wasn't healthy for him and the lifestyle that he was living. It wasn't a good time for him, so I wasn't surprised.

We're good friends. I think we became a lot closer to each other over the past 25-30 years. I think we've both experienced friendships that didn't work out that well and some that stayed with us for a long time. I think we learned from those, and we appreciate that we have each other. We appreciate that we have our friendship and we can openly talk about anything. When Marián needs some advice or I do, we just sometimes call each other to ask questions or opinions and it's always helpful. I think there's a huge amount of respect for each other and what we went through and what we've done, and that's great when you have friends like that.

_____

Seventeen

I'm reminded of Pavol Demitra every year on my daughter Mia's birthday.

It was right before her birth in 2011 that Pavol died in a plane crash with the KHL team Lokomotiv. I can't believe it's already been 10-plus years since he's been gone. Pavol was more than four years older than me, but we became really close over the years. We were both from the same area and played in the NHL. He was such a likable person. He was always having fun and smiling. He had a good attitude, told great jokes, and people just wanted to be around him. He had such a positive energy.

Pavol and I clicked because of our personalities. He enjoyed life on and off the ice. There was always a lot of laughs with him. When we went to the World Championships or Olympics, everyone looked forward to it because of Pavol.

We were usually roommates, and people would come to our room because we were always laughing. Everyone wanted to be a part of that. It was never boring around him.

Demo especially liked to play jokes on our friend and teammate Marián Gáborík. He knew how to get to Gabby. I remember at the Olympics he and I shared a room, and Gabby and Marcel shared another room, and we had some common area. Every morning, Demo would yell the first moment he saw Gabby. He pretended like the sight of Gabby scared him. It became a running joke and we looked forward to it every morning. He'd also tell Gabby that he looked like his father but just three years younger. We all laughed. Gabby had fun with it too. Pavol made the atmosphere so laid back. He was like

Gabby, Pavol, and I in our Slovakian team jerseys

that wherever he went. I remember talking to Keith Tkachuk about him when we played in Atlanta, because he and Keith became close while playing together in St. Louis. Pavol was just such a likable person.

Gabby did sort of get back at Pavol in a way. Demo had played with the Kings during the 2005–06 season. He and his family were really happy in Los Angeles. That next offseason, he was back in Slovakia. He and his wife, Maja, and Jana and I were driving home from a party at my parents' house one night in June. It had been a fun night. It was late, after midnight, and his phone began ringing. It was like, who would be calling him at this hour? He looked at the number and saw it was from the U.S. He's like, no way. He was worried. His wife told him to pick up. He said, no, I don't want to pick it up. Finally, he picked it up.

He's like, hello? And then he didn't say anything. We knew something was happening. It was a really short call and he hung up.

He's like, fuck, I just got traded.

His wife was almost crying. She's like, where did you get traded?

He said, Minnesota.

They were going from L.A., where the kids were wearing shorts and they had a nice setup, to Minnesota, where it was going to be minus whatever degrees.

He's like, "Fucking Gabby."

Gabby was one of the top players for Minnesota, so they would have asked him about Pavol and playing with him at Dukla Trenčín and on the national team. They probably thought he'd be a good teammate for Gabby. I remember how quiet it was in the car after that and how upset they were about leaving L.A. We got back to the apartment, and Pavol was just walking around and taking deep breaths. He couldn't believe it.

Another story about Pavol: he and I were approached by Orange, which is a major phone company in Slovakia, about doing a commercial prior to the 2007 World Championship. They wanted us to be a figuring skating duo. We thought they were joking at first. We went to the arena for the commercial shoot, and they actually had figure skating clothes for us and explained how they wanted us to dance and skate. I just couldn't imagine how it was going to look. But you know, we did a pretty decent job. And for the jumps, they brought in real figure skaters. We worked with the same company again years later and did a shoot with Marcel and Gabby. That was a lot of fun too. There were a lot of laughs. That Orange contract was pretty good. It only recently expired.

I loved playing with Pavol because he was so creative. We played give-and-go hockey, and that was fun to be a part of. We scored a lot of goals together. He loved to compete at the highest level. We both had that same feeling. We played together for the national team, but we also played a season together for our local team, Dukla Trenčín, during the 2004–05 lockout season. He and I played on a line together. Gabby would get thrown on our line when we really needed a goal and we also all played on the power play together.

I played with Pavol at the Olympics in 2010 and then in the World Championship in 2011. Those were my last two times playing with him. He led the Olympics in 2010 with 10 points and I finished second with nine points. We played well in that tournament. Unfortunately, we lost to Finland in the bronze game. That was disappointing.

In 2011, the Blackhawks lost in the first round of the playoffs, and I decided to play in the World Championship. The tournament was in Slovakia for the first time, and it was a big deal. Pavol had played in Russia that season and came home to play in the tournament. I was really looking forward to it. It was going to be a great atmosphere back home. It was a huge deal for us to host the tournament for the first time. But for some reason, we were really tight and couldn't do anything right on the ice. We lost to Germany in the first game, and that was devastating. That's a team we usually beat. We started getting criticized right away after that and couldn't bounce back. We didn't even get out of our group and make the playoffs. That was really hard to swallow. We fell way short of our expectations, and the players in that dressing room felt like we had let our whole country down. I felt sick to my stomach.

Before our last game, Pavol and I took a drive to Trenčín, which is one hour from Bratislava, and went to see our families. We felt like we didn't even want to drive back to the capital, but it was important to us to finish that last game with pride. Prior to that game, Pavol announced he was retiring from the national team. We beat Denmark in that game, and the whole arena was clapping and cheering for him, and he had tears in his eyes. It was amazing to see this national hero say goodbye to all those people. Nobody knew a few months later he'd be involved in this tragedy. I still have goosebumps thinking about it. He was so huge in the Slovakian hockey world.

THAT FALL, PAVOL went back to play for Lokomotiv in the KHL. A lot of the local NHL players had already flown to North America to join their training camps. I had stayed home because Jana was pregnant and was expecting our first baby any day. Two days before Mia was born, we got the news about Pavol. It was September 7, and I was at my sports center holding a charity program for kids. Someone told me what they heard had happened. I couldn't believe it. One of the reporters I knew called me and gave me the news. I was in disbelief. I just kept telling myself, this can't be right.

No one was sure if Pavol was definitely on the plane. He was dealing with an injury to his groin at that time, so we didn't know if he would have joined the team on the flight or stayed back due to his injury. But I started getting more and more calls, and the news started coming across the radio and TV. You began to realize that it might be true. I was trying to gather as much info as possible from everyone I knew.

Later, it was confirmed Pavol was on the plane that crashed. I had also known Brad McCrimmon, who was on the flight. I had him in Atlanta and Detroit as an assistant coach. He was a great guy, and I loved him as a coach. I had talked to Demo just a few days before that about the upcoming season and playing for McCrimmon, and McCrimmon and I talked before that season about how he might have an offer to coach in Russia. I had also played with Karel Rachůnek in Ottawa and had known Josef Vašíček. I couldn't believe it—there were four people I knew that were on that plane. It was just terrible, terrible news.

It was so devastating when we found out Pavol was definitely in the crash. I went to see his wife, Maja, a few days later. There were obviously lots of tears. It was a tough time. And then two days later, my daughter Mia was born. There were so many ups and downs in that period. It was difficult to deal with. You didn't know whether to celebrate or not. It all happened within a few days, these two major events. You had a close friend die tragically and then you had the best moment of your life with your first daughter being born. It was a difficult time to have all those feelings at the same time. I remember taking a walk from the hospital and thinking about everything. I didn't know how to react.

They held a service for Pavol shortly after that. Some of the guys flew back from their NHL camps for the funeral. I had stayed in Trenčín. I talked to the Blackhawks and arrived at camp later. The funeral was held at the Dukla Trenčín arena, which is now named after Demo. It was a big funeral and a nice service, but it was a really difficult experience.

On the 10-year anniversary of his death, I drove over to the cemetery where he is buried. It's not far from where I live. I dropped my daughter off at school, parked the car, and walked over to his grave. I brought a candle and just spent some time there alone. I reminded myself how fragile life can be. You can have everything one day and lose it the next. I obviously missed my really good friend. I said some prayers for Demo and hoped he was looking down on us from up there.

GABBY WAS CLOSE with Demo too. This is what he had to say about Pavol.

Marián Gáborík

As a hockey player, first, Pavol was a very intelligent player. He was very skilled. I don't know many players who had the hockey sense he had. As a person, he had that right kind of confident attitude that made him successful. He was always kind of the head of the clan in terms of getting people together for different functions. We loved being around him. He was a family guy. We got very close.

On the ice, we created a line with me, him, and Marián. On the international level, we were dominating games a lot. Obviously for me and Marián, we got unlucky on that international level that we weren't any part of those medals that Slovakia had won. It's kind of unfortunate, but at the end of the day, we always enjoyed playing for the national team, and we created a great chemistry with the guys around here, both on and off the ice. We had so much fun hanging out. In the Olympics in Vancouver, we shared four connected rooms with me, Pavol, Marián, and Marcel. We'd also group with other guys in our room at night and just talk. Everybody wanted to be around him.

When the accident occurred, I was in New York. We were having one of those skates before camp. I was just getting dressed and people told me what happened. I checked my phone. I couldn't believe it. I still got dressed and went on the ice. The reality hit me after five minutes on the ice and I went to sit on the bench. I just left and started checking if it was true. I was devastated.

I jumped on a plane and flew back to Slovakia. He got what he deserved in terms of people remembering him. He was huge. It's been 10 years now. Marián's daughter was born two days later. It's so interesting how life can be. One day you're losing one of your best friends, and then two days later probably one of the most memorable experiences in life is happening. I just don't know how Marián felt.

Even though Pavol wasn't technically from Trenčín, he was from Dubnica, maybe 10 miles away, and he started playing here before he went to the NHL. He then came back and was one of the owners of the club. He became a captain of the national team. In 2011 after the World Championship that we kind of messed up here in Slovakia, he was retiring from the national team and was very emotional after that game against Denmark. That last game, they could see the emotions he was expressing during that time, and he really kind of grew in people's hearts. And then it just multiplied.

The big funeral they had for him was amazing. It was televised and all the people showed up. He became a legend. They named the rink after him and they still remember him. Whenever the game is in the 38th minute, fans will keep clapping for the whole minute to honor his jersey number. Even if there's a break, people will keep clapping through the break until the minute of play is up. It's been 10 years, but people still cherish him that way.

Eighteen

I don't even think I really understood what the Hockey Hall of Fame was when I first visited it.

I went to Toronto with my Slovakia team as a 12- or 13-year-old for a tournament, and the trip actually started off terribly. We were supposed to be picked up at the airport and we were going to stay with some local families, but no one showed up. We sat at the airport for hours and ended up paying for a cheap motel ourselves. I remember I had 300 dollars from my parents to buy something from Canada, and I had to use 100 of it to pay for the motel, and it wasn't even our fault. There were a bunch of kids in one room and it was just chaos. The tournament organizers and our team staff definitely messed up big time.

After the first or second day, there was a Slovakian guy named Jaro Zec who lived in Toronto and had heard about our situation. He knew my dad from playing with him in the Czechoslovakian league. Jaro took in two of us to live with him for the week. He took us out to dinners, got us tickets to a Red Wings–Maple Leafs game, and just watched after us. It was such a great experience to go to a National Hockey League game. I remember him also taking us to McDonald's. That was a big deal, because we didn't have that back in Slovakia. I still keep in touch with him to this day because I'll never forget what he did for me back then. He and his family really made that trip memorable despite how it started.

We went to the Hall of Fame on that trip. I don't remember a whole lot about it, to tell you the truth. I remember seeing a lot of trophies. I was excited to see the Stanley Cup. I had watched the Final with Marcel, so the Cup was really cool to see in person. I knew some of the names in the Hall of Fame, but there were a lot that I didn't recognize because I was so young and didn't get a chance to watch a lot of those players. I don't think I really comprehended what the Hockey Hall of Fame was. I was just happy to take a picture with the Stanley Cup. Now, that's all obviously changed. Having a chance to go to the Hockey Hall of Fame back then and then return in 2021 as an inductee, it makes it all the more special.

I never thought about being selected for the Hockey Hall of Fame until late in my playing career. Toward the end in Chicago, there were people in the media or elsewhere that began saying I might have a Hall of Fame career with 1,000 games, more than 500 goals, and three Stanley Cups. I always thought that would be amazing, but it was for other people to judge whether my career was worthy of the Hall of Fame, not me. I had learned over the course of my career not to worry about the things I couldn't control. I could only control the way I played. If I ever got selected, that would obviously be incredible. For me, I just wanted to be remembered as a player who played the game the right way, who competed, and was multi-dimensional. I didn't want to be thought of as just a goal scorer, like that's all I do. Don't get me wrong, I loved scoring goals, but that wasn't all I did. I hope people remember me as a two-way player who played the game the right way.

I honestly didn't know what the rules were for being chosen to the Hall of Fame, especially with how I ended my career due to my skin condition. I didn't know if I could be selected three years after ending my career, or if it was necessary for my contract to officially be done. I thought the criteria might have been stricter, but I was humbled to be voted in the first year I was eligible. I still can't believe that it happened.

On the day I found out, my agent told me the call could happen between certain times in Slovakia. We had dinner that night, put the kids to bed, and then I was doing something on my computer. It was getting late. All of a sudden, my phone started to ring. I looked at the phone and it was a Toronto area code. I picked it up and it was Lanny McDonald from the Hockey Hall of Fame. I thought, well, they wouldn't call me if I wasn't selected. But you still want to hear it with your own ears. I heard his voice and he told me he was excited to share the great news.

I was speechless. My whole career flashed before my eyes. I didn't cry, but I was emotional. When Jana heard me say something in English, she ran toward the office and she had tears in her eyes. It was special. We opened a bottle of wine. It was a phone call I will never forget.

The next morning, the kids woke up and we sat them down and told them exactly what happened. I'm not sure if they really understood. They're like, cool, whatever. They were seven and nine.

I HAD TO wait for the actual ceremony, due to COVID. They delayed it until November of 2021, but I was fine with that. It was special just getting in.

When the time finally came, the five days in Toronto went by fast. There was so much on the schedule for the six induct-ees, which included Ken Holland, Jarome Iginla, Kevin Lowe, Kim St-Pierre, Doug Wilson, and myself. I told myself going into it that it all would be something new and to try to enjoy every day. I kept telling myself that before every event. There was so much to do and so many people watching you, it's hard not to be nervous. But I just smiled and tried to enjoy it, because I realized that this doesn't happen for a lot of people, and I was lucky. It was great, too, because I brought along 14 people, including friends and family.

The first day, we had a ceremony at the Hockey Hall of Fame where they gave us our rings. We had pictures taken and talked to the media. The rings were cool because they were so different from the Stanley Cup rings I had. The color of the ring was different, but it was also smaller, which actually is nice. I can probably wear it around if I wanted. The Stanley Cup rings are too huge to wear. Later that day, we went to Scotiabank Centre and were introduced to the crowd before the Flames-Leafs game. They put down a carpet for us to get out onto the ice, but it was blue, not red, because blue is the color of the Leafs. Everyone got their own suite for their families. It was really great because it was my daughter Zoja's birthday, and we brought her a cake and presents into the suite. That was special for her and us. It was fun to be at a live NHL game, too, as I hadn't been to one in some years. We weren't able to interact with the players because of COVID protocols, but I saw Jason Spezza, who I had played with in Ottawa, and he said congratulations, which was nice to hear. I told him it was good to see that he was still kicking with the young guys.

The next day was the Legends Classic game. I hadn't skated or worn any equipment for nearly four years, and I thought it was going to be a lot worse than it was. It took me a bit to get into it, but eventually I started feeling pretty good. I was holding the puck, making plays, and having fun. It definitely brought some memories back. It was special after not having that feeling for four years. I was able to have Marcel play in the game too. It made for some great memories and pictures. I think it was nice for my daughters as well. My wife even said their eyes lit up with me skating on the ice and going by the glass. It's different than when they were younger. It was amazing for my family to see me in a different way. I think they enjoyed it a lot.

Wearing the equipment didn't bother my skin the way it did before I retired. We didn't put on the shoulder pads, because we didn't really have to; no one was going to hit anybody in this type of game. Plus, we didn't sweat much. It was a slow game. But playing with Mike Modano and John LeClair on a line was a great experience. We were moving pretty good, and the goals were decent. The game speed was obviously way slower than a regular NHL game. I did back-check for fun once. I was following a guy and waiting for the right moment to take the puck, but I didn't know who the guy was, and I didn't feel exactly right about taking it from him. It was fun, though. Before the game, we were given our Hall of

Fame blazers. The game had started, and Jarome Iginla and I had to run to the dressing room and join them for the second half.

My buddy Andy had set us up at a steak house after the game for a nice dinner with my family and friends. We invited Nick Lidström, because he had flown over with his wife to present me. We also invited Dominik Hašek, who was a client of my agent Ritch Winter, and Marshall Johnston, who had drafted me in Ottawa. It was a beautiful setup in one of the top restaurants in Toronto, and I was able to enjoy the time with my family and friends. The food and drinks were fantastic. I couldn't have pictured it any better.

But then something better did happen: Lanny McDonald showed up at like 10 p.m. with the Stanley Cup. We got to enjoy it for an hour. That was so cool and unexpected. We took a lot of pictures and videos with the Cup. Plus, my friends from the party in Trenčín got to see the Cup in a better condition than the last time it had left our city. The Hockey Hall of Fame took it after an hour and joked that it wouldn't be falling down any stairs that night. We all had a good laugh. That was such a surprise and so nice of them.

The night before that I got together with some Blackhawks teammates: Brent Seabrook, Kris Versteeg, Bryan Bickell, and Andrew Shaw. Dave Bolland was going to come, too, but he got sick. There were five us and we talked for hours. It felt like we had a game the next day. It was like nothing had changed. We had a great time. No one wanted to go home, everyone wanted to keep talking and feeling good about seeing each other again. When it was time to leave, the guys jumped in Ubers, but the Uber for Seabs and me didn't arrive, so we went back to the bar and grabbed a couple more quick drinks.

As a group, we obviously talked about what was going on with the Blackhawks regarding the alleged assault of Kyle Beach. I really didn't know what happened with him in 2010. When I heard about the allegations initially, I called Kopy and asked him if I was losing my mind, because I didn't recall anything about what was alleged. What happened is disturbing. The Blackhawks' independent report was difficult to read. I'm glad it has been addressed by the Blackhawks. People obviously have lost their jobs over it. There were a lot of people with character in that room back then. I want to believe that if we knew at the time that something had happened, we would have come out about it. I know there are some players who are saying everyone knew, but that's simply not true. My question is, if those two players knew, why didn't they tell anyone? I can't change what people want to think, I can only tell you what I knew, and that is what I told the investigators.

We were going to have my Legacy Night ceremony with the Blackhawks right around the Hockey Hall of Fame induction. My family and friends were going to fly into Chicago for that as well. I was looking forward to it and it seemed like perfect timing. But when the report came out, I started feeling like it was a bad idea. As it got closer, I felt like it just wasn't right to do. We set up a call with the Blackhawks and we agreed to postpone it. Both sides felt it wasn't the right time to celebrate anything. I felt good about that, and I was happy Danny Wirtz and the organization felt the same way.

THE FINAL DAY at the Hockey Hall of Fame was the ceremony where I would give my speech. I was still working on it that morning. It was longer than I expected as I read it and kept rehearsing it. Ritch helped me with the speech, as he had done when we started working on it together a couple months earlier. Big thanks to my agent for that. We had done a run-through at the location in the morning. I wanted to read it off my papers instead of the teleprompter. I went back to my room and worked on it some more, just with my English and trying to memorize it. The rest of my family took a walk around Toronto, so I was in my room by myself. Like in the movies, I was standing in front of the mirror reading it to myself. Even as I was doing that, I was getting emotional and actually brought some tears to my eyes, which as you know doesn't happen much.

After that, I was talking to one of my Canadian friends. He knew about speeches quite a bit and walked me through a few things. He asked if I put anything in the speech in my native language, Slovak. I told him I hadn't. I had thought about it, but it seemed better to just speak in English. He told me that I really should and that I would regret it if I didn't. I started working on something on my iPad after we hung up and printed it out. I read it during the speech and thanked a

Giving my speech at the Hockey Hall of Fame ceremony

number of people and my hometown team in Slovak, and I'm glad I did. It felt really good to do:

> Teší ma a som hrdý na to, že ako tretí hráč z malého Slovenska a krásneho mesta Trenčin som to dotiahol až tu, do veľkého Toronta do Siene Slávy.
>
> Veľmi by som chcel poďakovať Slovenskému hokeju a všetkým trénerom národného tímu, ktorí ma trénovali.
>
> Hlavne by som rad poďakoval mojim trénerom Dukly Trenčin bez ktorých by toto nebolo možné.
>
> Tréneri Bakoš, Opatovsky, Mikušik, Bratranec, Boldiš, Šinkovič, Bohunicky, Novotny, Čecho, Matušek, Poč, Walter, Hiadlovsky.
>
> Veľká vďaka.

I had Nick Lidström introduce me. Since none of my Blackhawks teammates were in the Hall of Fame yet, I thought about Lidström and playing with him in Detroit. He was a role model on and off the ice. I thought it would be great to receive the plaque from someone like him. I knew he was in Sweden. I called him to see what he was doing in November. I told him there was no pressure in doing it, but I would be honored if he could. He said he was actually going to be in Detroit, but that he'd talk to his wife. He took a day or two and texted me that he'd be glad to come. I was so happy. For him to come to Toronto, that was really special.

Once I got on stage, I wasn't that nervous. Like before, I told myself to keep smiling and enjoy it. I was pretty calm during the speech. I wouldn't say it was perfect, but I thought it went well enough. When I watched it again a few days later, I thought I had done well considering I hadn't been in North America for a few years. I also got to see what it was like on the broadcast. As I was talking, they had pictures of Trenčín, the castle, and my teammates. That was pretty cool. There were also closeups of my parents and my wife. My mom and Jana had tears in their eyes. That was great to capture those moments.

We drove back to the hotel after the Hockey Hall of Fame event and Ritch and I met with Danny Wirtz, Jaime Faulkner, and Kyle Davidson from the Blackhawks. We met for a couple of hours and I was impressed by what they said. I had a good feeling about the meeting and the plan they had for the future. They had a lot on their plate with everything going on, but they seemed prepared, and I liked what I heard. The plan was to continue to talk in the future.

I gave myself an extra day in Canada with my family. We went to my friend's house and had dinner there. It was nice because all the stress was behind me. The next day we flew home from Toronto to Vienna and drove to Trenčín. Coming home, I had a good feeling about the week and everything that had happened. I hadn't been sure I was going to enjoy the experience. It was overwhelming when I saw the list of everything I was scheduled to do. But as soon as I got there, it all worked out. The Hockey Hall of Fame was incredible. I have a lot of great memories from that week. Everything was *almost* perfect: I tested positive for COVID when I got home, as did a lot of my family. But everyone was vaccinated and had mild symptoms, so that wasn't too bad either.

NICK LIDSTRÖM TALKED to Scott about joining me for my Hockey Hall of Fame induction and having played together for a season in Detroit. I'm grateful he was willing to fly in and introduce me.

Nicklas Lidström

We only played together for a year, but it was nice to get the call from him. It's quite an honor that he called me. You would think maybe he would talk to one of his fellow countrymen or maybe an old coach or maybe another player that's played with him for a long time, so I was thrilled when I got the call from him.

I remember after we won the Cup the first time in '08, Ken Holland called me in the summertime. He said we've just signed Hossa to a one-year deal, he wanted to come to us. And so, that was super exciting to have a chance to play with him, having just faced him a couple months earlier and knowing how good of a player he was. I was really thrilled that he wanted to join our team and be part of our team, so I was looking forward to that training camp.

Playing against him, he was always highly skilled, really strong on the puck, got a great shot, and he could really skate out there. We were in the Western Conference at the time, and they were in the Eastern Conference, the teams he was on, so we didn't face him a whole lot. But then when I got a chance to play with him, you realize he's just as good defensively. He's a hard worker, backchecks real hard, real responsible defensively, and his overall work ethic was phenomenal. His 200-foot game was better than you thought when you played against him. You don't really see that. You see the offense when you're facing him. But he was just as good defensively too.

I think he probably saw how hard Pavel [Datsyuk] worked, what kind of player he was. Hossa, being a smart player himself, took all the different pieces from different players. From Pavel, he saw the work ethic from him. And there are a lot of similarities to the two players because both had that unbelievable skill set as well. He could deke and beat guys, but as far as work ethic, I think Hossa was just as hard a worker as Pavel was. You can tell that he wanted to be that 200-foot player that Pav was.

I remember being around [Steve] Yzerman and Chelios and guys older than me. You looked up to them, and you saw the experience that they brought into the locker room. With the veteran team that we had, you can add [Kris] Draper, [Kirk] Maltby, the hard-working guys to the mix. It's about knowing how to be a pro. We can go out and have a glass of wine at dinner and we can enjoy ourselves, but when we were in the locker room and when there was a game going to be played or practice, we were focused on what we were supposed to do. I think he learned a lot from our veteran group, that you can relax and have a good time and all that, but when it really matters, when it's gametime or you have to be focused, we were focused. So I think he learned a lot from being around veteran players and guys that had just reached the Final and just won the Stanley Cup. I think he learned from the way we acted as a group.

Him being a low-key guy, a fun guy to be around, we went out for dinners on a lot of occasions during the year and played golf in training camp and just hung out, so I really enjoyed his company. He led on the ice, setting an example by the way he played. Maybe not being a vocal guy in the room; it's kind of hard coming into a new room, a new team, and trying to be a leader right away when we had that veteran presence on our team. But I thought he led by example on the ice, his work ethic and being the game changer he could be, whether it's scoring goals or blocking shots, doing the little things. What sticks out the most is the way he could score goals from out of nowhere. He could find an open spot or get a shot through with that quick wrister that he had. He helped our team have success and go to the Final that year he was with us.

Having known the disappointments he had been through two years in a row being in the Final and having a chance to win the Cup and coming up short, I think he learned a lot from those years, what it took to go all the way. Having been there before, you know the extra effort or whatever it is you need to get over the hump. I was happy that he finally won a Cup, especially after two disappointing years like that.

I really enjoyed [being at the Hall of Fame with him]. I was there in 2015, so it's been a few years, but I know the excitement of the whole weekend. You have your family or friends around you. You're super excited to be a part of the Hall of Fame weekend. You get treated really nice by the Hall. Everything leading up to that Monday when you're actually getting inducted into the Hall of Fame, it's such a wonderful and fun weekend. So I knew what he was going through and the excitement that he was going through. I know he earned the right to do that, and I was happy to see him go through that too.

Nineteen

Early on in my career, I wasn't thinking much about investing or owning anything back home in Slovakia. As I got older, I decided I wanted to give something back to the communities where I grew up. I just wasn't sure which direction to go.

My business partner Miro Kubis and I had an idea. I wanted to build something and invest some money in the city where I live with my family, and so Miro went to meet the mayor of Trenčín to discuss that. Our newly established company purchased some land from the city during the middle of my playing career when I was in my mid-20s. The land was in an older area of town, and Miro knew there were plans for a new bridge that would make this location very attractive. Slowly, we began to create a plan and visualize what we could build there.

I met Miro a long time ago. He's from Trenčín too. I believe we met through someone in hockey. When I changed financial planners, he had started to work with my new advisors in North America and it was good to have somebody to be able to explain certain things in my language. We became better friends and then he brought some interesting ideas to the table, and we became business partners.

We wanted to create a multi-sport recreation center for everyone in the city, from small children to senior citizens. There were some old clay tennis courts already on the

My very good friends Big Pete and Miro have helped plan our Stanley Cup celebration parties back home

property we purchased from the city. We started renovating the rest. We built a clubhouse with a restaurant and changed the surface to artificial grass to accommodate more sports. Later on, we looked out from the terrace and thought it would be nice to acquire nearby land so that our sport center could expand. However, the other part of the land was in a flooded area, and you couldn't build anything there. We went to see the mayor and the council with a new idea for expansion. We promised to invest more than 1 million euros there. We told them we'd like to build a small, nine-hole executive golf course and beach area. It wouldn't be for any construction of houses or anything similar. They were resistant at first, because golf hadn't existed here during the socialist times, but we did a lot of work on our presentation and explained that we would promote a healthy lifestyle; that children would play for 1 euro; and that we would have advantageous programs for senior citizens—which we do today, and many older citizens of Trenčín are now happy members. So eventually they came around to it. I was already playing golf in North America, and there weren't many golf courses at that time in Slovakia.

People didn't know what was going on with the land because we had bulldozers over there. They knew I owned the land and was going to build something, but they weren't sure what. We commissioned a professional golf course designer to create the course. Miro had known him for many years and persuaded him to do a charity course to grow the game of golf in Slovakia, since he had been very successful and did many PGA Tour golf courses. He didn't put his name on it, because it wasn't a traditional 18-hole course, but he did us a favor and designed our nine-hole course and sent us a very good shaper from Scotland. It was crazy seeing the bulldozer work on the site. He was doing things you've never seen before. He was moving so fast and shaping the course very nicely and turning the abandoned area into a very nice

A view of the Hoss Sport Center and my nine-hole golf course in Trenčín

golf course. People were wondering, what the hell is he doing over there?

Eventually, people in the city saw what we did and how we were trying to make the area nicer. Families could come and play golf and go to the beach area. I just wanted to build up something meaningful for the citizens in the city I grew up in and improve the quality of life. Marián Gáborík had already built a hockey rink. It would probably be too much if I did another rink, so I decided to go in a different direction and built a multi-sport facility for people here. When we moved back from Chicago, my wife also opened a very nice yoga and Pilates studio as a part of our sport center.

It took some time for people to get used to the sport center. Even the tennis courts, it took a while for people to get accustomed to them. Everybody's nosy. They're like, what's going on? Then, they're back to their old habits. It was the same thing with the restaurant at the golf course. You really have to be patient with certain things in life. Even with the apartment building that we sold to a developer, they sold slowly and then they picked up, and today it is one of the best addresses in town. Eventually, if the product is good, the people will come to it. You have to be patient. We have even more members for the golf course now and more people are using the facilities. It makes me very happy to have done something good for the city I live in.

It helps having my name associated with the business, but you still need quality. You could have Wayne Gretzky's name on a pack of food, but if it doesn't taste good, no one's going to buy it. You need to have some quality you're offering to people. Whether it's the golf course or tennis courts, they have to be in good shape. If people are paying for something, they want something in return. It's all about quality of service, and that's important to me. When I do something, I want it to be just like when I was on the ice. I want to do it 100 percent. That's how I went about the golf course. Even with my wife's yoga studio, it could be simpler, but I told her when people come here, I want to make them feel relaxed. Same thing with the golf course, I want them to have a nice and relaxing walk. People want to get away from their everyday lives. I believe there are many healthy benefits for people when they come to play our golf course. It's just nine holes, but you can turn off your brain a little bit, get some energy, and relax with the beautiful views of the castle and Váh River. It's important for me when I have my stamp on it, that there's a little more quality to it.

I like to play golf myself too. I've won our golf club's championship a few times. I won the big tournament twice and then our match-play tournament another two times. In 2021, I lost both of them, which is probably good because I don't want people to feel like I'm winning all the time here. I didn't build the golf course for just myself.

Last year, I did land a hole in one. It was the second one in club history. We were on the fourth hole, which is about 130 meters long. I just swung the club and the ball hit the pin. We heard the noise and saw the flag was shaking. I couldn't see the ball, so I thought there was a chance. It was during a tournament, and I was playing with a doctor I knew a little bit. He played his ball next and then I went behind the hole to see if I could locate my ball. I didn't see it anywhere. I'm like, I'm going to look in the hole. And there was the ball. I was like, no way. I told the doctor I felt like I scored my first NHL goal. It was that same feeling. I joked that I was waiting for this longer than my first Stanley Cup. I'm glad someone was there to see it because no one was going to believe me otherwise. I am glad that our marshal was there to witness it too. He took a picture of me for my first hole in one.

BACK IN 2005 or 2006, my cousin had owned a restaurant. It was a typical Slovak restaurant. He was making these pierogi from my grandmother's recipe. She was my mom's mom. It's called *stará mama*, which means grandmother in Slovak. People really liked them, and the restaurant began filling up. My cousin started selling the pierogi to other restaurants. He wanted to turn that into a business and distribute food to other restaurants. He pitched the idea to me. At first, I wasn't interested. I was just concentrating on hockey. After a few years, I was making more money and decided to invest in it. I figured people were always going to have to eat. It was something totally different for me. In 2008, we both put up some money and created our business. It was called HO&PE. It was the first two letters of my last name and the first two letters of his last name. You can read it as HOPE, but it was HO and PE.

The company was growing quickly, but then we started having more and more problems. The business started sinking a bit. I wasn't paying too much attention to it. I was focused on hockey. I didn't want to go to the rink and worry about

Putting my name on our building after we rebranded my firm in east Slovakia

something else. I always said that I was more an investor than a business partner.

Since I stopped playing in 2017, I've put more attention into the business. Things hadn't been going as I was told. That was a red flag for me, and we had to make some major changes. I took over the company, bought my cousin's shares, and we started making those changes. There were competitors who wanted to buy the company for cheap. The sharks smelled blood. I could have maybe sold it and been done with it. The other option was hiring the right people to run it. I had family members working for the company and I didn't just want to sell it and lay them off. I felt some responsibility. I bought out my cousin and put even more money into it. We rebranded the company in 2021 and renamed it Hossa Family.

I really got involved in the rebranding and marketing of the company. If I wanted the company to succeed, I had to understand and really learn about it. I took that on and began cultivating my own vision for it. We also hired the right people around me. Now we have 250 employees, over 60 automobiles and 50 distribution vehicles, four warehouses, and seven logistic depots. It's a big process, but I feel like we're going in the right direction. We distribute all types of food. We have 3,500 stock items, including our products like pierogi, sweet dumplings, patties, and other traditional pastas. In addition, we offer chilled meat products like steaks, chicken breasts, and so on. We're also selling frozen produce and can supply restaurants and hotels with any type of food, whatever they need. It's a one-stop shop for restaurants.

This has obviously been something totally different for me to get into it. I never thought I'd be involved in a food distribution business. When I first started, I had no idea what I was doing. It was like swimming in the middle of the ocean. But I slowly started talking to people and finding people who knew what to do. I feel like it's all about the people around you. When you surround yourself with quality people, good things happen. We went through some rough times, but that's how we got better. It's just like sports. People show their true character when things get tough. That's how we won championships. I try to bring that personality and attitude to the company. I came at it from a hockey perspective. Whether things are going well or not, I try to bring the discipline I learned from playing hockey to the company. It's good to see where the company is now. I was driving in Bratislava in October of 2021 and saw our new logo on a truck, and it felt really good. We have a lot of work ahead of us, but we're turning things around.

I was always pretty good with my money. I was never one of those guys to spend a crazy amount. If you can't afford something, easy—just don't buy it. I always made sure we were in a good position financially. It's also a different lifestyle back here than it is the U.S. I've always tried to be careful. I'd rather spend wisely and try to build something and leave some legacy behind me.

ASIDE FROM MY role in my company, I've also picked up boxing since retiring from hockey. I continued to work out and stay in shape, because that's what I love to do. That's my lifestyle. I was working out with Marcel one day and told him I was getting bored. I was doing the same things my whole career. I wanted to do something new. I knew a guy who was teaching boxing. It's like when I started skiing. I had never skied before and picked it up. My brother asked if he could come along. We bought a pair of boxing gloves and started learning to box.

It was boring in the beginning, but it was important to learn the fundamentals and not pick up any bad habits. It's now been two-plus years since we started doing it and I really love the sport. I have a lot of respect for boxers and MMA fighters. They really have to watch their weight and train really hard, just like us hockey players, but the big difference is they are in the cage alone. No teammates, just on their own. There's nobody they can hide behind. We're lucky in a team sport, because everybody has a bad day but your teammates can pick up the slack and no will know. With an individual sport, there's no room for error. Plus, you have to be in top shape to get through all the rounds and, more importantly, you have to be strong in your head. Confidence is everything. When I first started sparring, I'd go through three or four rounds and I was dying. I was like, wow, now I know how those guys feel. You can have all the talent, but if you don't have the cardio, you are done.

I have never been knocked out. We figured out early on that it's best to hit heavy low and lighter high. We wear helmets, but we don't punch too hard in the head anyway. There was a guy who I sparred who tried to hit me, I ducked, and he fell down because he had swung so hard. I was like, what happened? He started grabbing his knee because he hurt his MCL. Soon after that, another guy sparred me in his bare feet. I went to punch him, and he went down before I hit him. Again, I'm like, what happened again? He got the nail in his foot stuck in the ground. The trainer was like, Hoss, you can't fight anybody else because you're beating everybody up, your last two sparring partners went down not because of KO punches, but because of luck. We couldn't stop laughing.

The boxing is more for cardio and getting a good sweat, but I have also learned how to protect myself if needed. I'm not saying it's going to happen on the street. I always tried to avoid fighting whenever challenged off the ice. People would try to fight me in a bar or something and I'd just walk away.

I don't want to get hurt, sued, or anything else. I still think that way, but at least now if something was to happen, I could protect myself.

I didn't have too many fights in the NHL. My first fight was against Vinny Lecavalier in 1999. We were both rookies. That was a quick one, but it was my first Gordie Howe hat trick. There was some scrum and we grabbed each other. He threw off his gloves, and I didn't know what to do. I ended up throwing my gloves, too, and was protecting myself and punching at the same time. I'm sure I looked funny. When I was with Atlanta, I fought Oleg Tverdovsky during the 2005–06 season and John Erskine during the 2006–07 season. I fought Nashville's Ryan Suter during the 2008–09 season, when I was with the Red Wings. I had to go against Suter because our line with Pavel Datsyuk was constantly facing him and Shea Weber of the Predators. I think Kenny Holland was surprised by me fighting. He told me that he never wanted to see me fighting again because he needed me to score goals, but he did say it was good to see I didn't mind throwing some punches. I still do think there should be fighting in hockey, I just think it should be the same or similar size guys going. I don't want Tom Wilson fighting some skilled guy. I don't think guys should be pressured to fight either. If two guys are willing to go, fine, let them go. These days it's like there's a big hit and people go, whoa, like all of a sudden somebody has to jump the guy who made the hit, even if it was a clean hit. There are some people who want to see fighting. It's entertainment for them. But there's a lot less fighting in the NHL now than there was early in my career.

Working out has been always important to me. I used to train twice a day in the offseason before we had kids. After the kids came, I tried to squeeze the two sessions into one. My wife asked me in the summer why I didn't practice less and spend more time doing other things. I told her I couldn't stop because I felt like I would be shorting myself. That's just how I am with certain things. If I was supposed to work out and I didn't, I probably wouldn't be able to sleep. It'd be in my head and bugging me so much. I just need to put a checkmark on that. That's how I was taught. I wanted to do it 100 percent. It only took 2-3 hours a day. That was my job and I enjoyed it. I never had to do the fitness testing with the Blackhawks. Joel told me he didn't care about the testing. He knew I was prepared. He could see I was lean and fit. When I jumped on the ice, he knew I was ready to go.

LIFE AFTER HOCKEY has been good. It's been a smooth transition. It helped that I invested some money during my career and have some things I can get involved with. I don't need to work 9-to-5 or whatever. I help with strategies and stay involved in the businesses, but I don't have to be there all the time. When things need to get done, I do them.

As for my hockey career, I do have one final story for you. This is an example of everything seeming to happen for a reason.

I was originally supposed to come to Chicago for the 10-year anniversary of our 2010 Stanley Cup championship, but then COVID halted that. And then, I was planning to be in Chicago around my Hall of Fame induction to be honored with a Legacy Night, but we decided to postpone that with everything going on with the organization. So, we planned again for early April of 2022, and the third time was the charm. I stayed a full week, and it was magical.

The week began with me being able to attend Jonathan Toews' 1,000th game ceremony. He had no idea I was coming in for it. I first saw his parents in the hallway of the United Center, and they were shocked to see me. I was there with Patrick Sharp, Brent Seabrook, and Andrew Shaw. Waiting in the tunnel to go onto the ice brought back so many memories of being there in that exact spot. It reminded me how special that was. We walked onto the ice behind Jonny from the bench. He was so surprised when he saw us. I was the last one out and handed him his silver stick for the milestone. To be there for that, to hear the United Center fans and not having been there for almost five years, it's one of those moments you'll never forget. After the game, I had some beers with him and his friends and there was a dinner for him the following night. It meant so much for me to be part of his celebration. We had been through so much together.

The week only got better from there. The main reason I was in town was to sign a one-day contract and officially retire with the Blackhawks. It was something I told the organization I wanted to do back when I allowed them to trade my contract to Arizona, and Rocky Wirtz was a man of his word. Chicago and the Blackhawks have such great meaning for my career, me personally, and for my family. I feel such a deep connection with the organization, so it was important to me to retire with the Blackhawks.

That would have been enough for me, but the Blackhawks went even further and told me they planned to retire my No. 81 jersey. I was blown away. I was speechless. They later announced it to the fans just after I signed my one-day contract. I'll be back in Chicago for that ceremony early in the 2022–23 season. I'm so grateful for the Blackhawks wanting to do that. I understand how rare and special that is. It's not why I played the game, but I'm honored Rocky and the Blackhawks felt I was deserving of that.

That night, I was in a United Center suite with my close friend Peter Neveriš, my agent Ritch Winter, and former teammates Richard Pánik and Michal Rozsíval. We were sitting there having a few beers, and I looked up at the jerseys and names the Blackhawks had already retired to the rafters. I just couldn't believe my name and number would be up there too. It's not something you ever think about. It's really an amazing feeling. I know that will be up there long after I'm gone. That will be part of my legacy. There aren't many players who have been given that honor, and I feel so lucky and grateful that it's happening to me. I couldn't have dreamed for a better ending to my hockey career.